AF664000

REBELS OF AURORIUM

Satya Nagam

Qurate
quratebooks.com

REBELS OF AURORIUM

Satya Nagam

Published in 2025

Qurate Books Pvt. Ltd.
Goa 403523, India
www.quratebooks.com
Tel: 1800-210-6527, Email: info@quratebooks.com

ISBN: 978-93-58980-78-3

With the Blessing of My Father
Nagam Khadar Chellaram

For the unwavering guidance, love, and strength you have imparted to me.
This work carries your wisdom, your courage, and the light of your blessings.

Preface

In the quiet corners of imagination, where reality and fantasy dance in delicate synchrony, this novel finds its genesis. As I sit down to pen these words, I am acutely aware of the privilege bestowed upon me – the privilege to create worlds, breathe life into characters, and embark on a journey where the boundaries of the ordinary blur into the extraordinary.

Within the pages that follow, readers will traverse landscapes both familiar and fantastical, as the narrative unfolds like the petals of a flower eager to reveal its innermost secrets. It is my sincere hope that this literary odyssey serves as a vessel, transporting you to realms uncharted, challenging preconceptions, and inviting contemplation on the myriad facets of the human experience.

Writing, for me, is an act of exploration – a venture into the recesses of the mind, a pilgrimage to the uncharted territories of emotion, and a quest to understand the complexities of the human spirit. Threads of inspiration have been woven from the myriad influences that have shaped my own perception of the world.

As you embark on this literary sojourn, I invite you to embrace the uncertainty, revel in the mysteries, and surrender to the ebb and flow of the story. Let the words weave their magic, for in the realm of fiction, the ordinary is extraordinary, and the mundane, sublime.

For every dreamer among the readers, for those finding solace in the written language, and for the inquisitive spirits prepared to journey through the intricate pathways of this story – thank you for embarking on this journey with me. May these pages be a sanctuary, and a mirror that resonates with the echoes of your own stories

Contents

1

The school

Aurorium City basked under a golden glow as Victoria and Henry Parker delved into an earnest conversation about their daughter's future. Little Ava, just two years old, had already become the center of their dreams, and they were intent on securing her place in the finest school the city had to offer.

Victoria, juggling her morning routine with clockwork precision, darted around the house, her heels clicking against the floor as time ticked away. Meanwhile, Henry, the picture of calm, stood by the kitchen counter, swirling his coffee with unhurried ease.

In the living room, Ava giggled, her tiny fingers reaching for her beloved toy. Her innocence painted a heartwarming contrast to her parents' aspirations, as though the whole world was unfolding at her little fingertips.

Victoria hastily dressed up in the bedroom, glancing at the clock with every other movement. She leaned back from her closet and called out, "Henry, have you looked into schools for Ava's admission? We need to make sure that Ava's skills match the requirements."

In the kitchen, Henry calmly poured coffee into a mug, the steam swirling up as he replied, "Yes, I have. I already submitted her genetic profile. We're waiting for the school's approval."

As she quickly fastened her earrings in front of the mirror, Victoria's movements were brisk and efficient. She said with a hint of worry, "I just hope that Ava has the right skills for the school."

Henry strolled into the living room, a steaming mug of coffee in hand. He sank onto the couch beside Ava, who was giggling and babbling as she clutched her favorite toy. Watching her tiny fingers explore, he glanced at Victoria with a calm smile. "Relax," he said reassuringly. "The school has everything they need. They'll evaluate Ava's abilities thoroughly before deciding. And if this doesn't work out, we'll find another path—always."

Victoria's heels clicked rhythmically against the floor as she approached, her bag swinging gently from her shoulder. She leaned down, planting a swift kiss on Henry's cheek and another on Ava's soft curls. "You're right," she murmured, masking her lingering doubts with a brave smile. "We just want the best for her, always."

As she rushed to the door, she called out, "See you guys, bye!" Henry gently held Ava's tiny hand and waved it, saying, "Say bye to Mama."

Victoria turned, her face softening into a smile as she replied, "Bye, sweetie." She gave one last look at her family, shut the door behind her, and dashed to her car, her mind already racing with thoughts of the busy day ahead.

Henry's home office was a perfect blend of simplicity and sophistication—a refined retreat where work and reflection seamlessly intertwined. Though modest in size, the room radiated tranquility, wrapped in a muted palette of soft grays and whites, enriched by warm wooden accents that infused the space with natural elegance.

The walls told a silent yet vivid story through a series of framed photographs, each carefully selected to celebrate Henry's cherished moments. One photo captured Victoria's radiant smile, her warm eyes brimming with the love they shared. Another showcased Henry and Ava in an unguarded moment of laughter during a family outing, her sparkling eyes and wide grin a testament to their unbreakable bond. The centerpiece was a large family portrait from a sunlit beach vacation, where Henry, Victoria, and Ava stood arm-in-arm, their joy practically leaping out of the frame. The understated wooden frames and neutral-toned photos harmonized effortlessly with the room's minimalist decor, infusing it with warmth and heart.

On one side, built-in shelves held a thoughtfully curated selection of books and mementos, reflecting Henry's personality and interests. Books were meticulously arranged by size and color, while select pieces of art and family photographs added layers of meaning. A single potted plant, with its vibrant green leaves, brought life and freshness to the otherwise serene space. The balance of form and function in every detail elevated the room, making it more than just an office—it was a sanctuary of stories, passions, and quiet inspiration.

The room was softly illuminated by contemporary floor lamp with a brushed steel finish. The window, dressed with sheer curtains, offered a tranquil view of the garden outside, bringing a sense of serenity to the office.

The centrepiece of the office was a sleek, minimalist desk made of polished walnut. At first glance, the desk appeared unassuming, almost like any other high-end piece of office furniture. But with a click of a discreet button embedded on its edge, it transformed into a hub of futuristic innovation.

The surface of the desk softly illuminated, casting a gentle glow that filled the room with a subtle, ambient light. This illumination was not just for show; it served a purpose.

As the desk lit up, a holographic display sprang to life, projected above the surface. The display was crisp and clear, hovering in mid-air and responding effortlessly to Henry's gestures. With a wave of his hand, he could navigate through files, open documents, and even conduct video calls. The holographic interface provided an expansive, multi-dimensional workspace, freeing him from the constraints of traditional monitors.

Beneath the holographic display, the desk itself became an interactive surface. A virtual keyboard illuminated on the smooth surface, the keys glowing with a soft white light. The desk's advanced technology was seamlessly integrated, with no visible wires or clunky hardware to detract from its sleek appearance. It embodied the perfect blend of form and function, a testament to innovative design and cutting-edge technology.

Henry himself was dressed comfortably yet casually, a testament to his laid-back approach to working from home. He wore a simple, well-fitted T-shirt that complemented his athletic build and a pair of casual shorts that allowed for ease of movement. His attire was practical and relaxed, perfectly suited for the informal environment of his home office.

In his hand, Henry held a steaming mug of coffee, its rich aroma filling the room. He took a sip, savoring the warmth and the burst of energy it provided, a small ritual that marked the start of his productive day.

The holographic display in front of him projected various reports, which he skimmed through before selecting one to share with the team. His colleagues' faces appeared in a grid on the display, each one focused on the task at hand.

"Alright, team," Henry began, leaning forward slightly, "let's dive into the code integration issues we've been facing. Any insights, Ana?"

Ana nodded, her expression serious. "Yes, Henry . It seems like there's a conflict in the modules when we try to merge the branches. We might need to re-evaluate the dependencies."

"Good catch, Ana," Henry replied, appreciating her attention to detail. "Mark, what's your take on this?"

Adjusting his glasses, Mark said, "I've been looking into it, and I think a restructuring of the codebase could help. We need to streamline the dependencies and re-factor some of the functions to avoid conflicts."

Henry nodded in agreement. "Great. Let's put together a plan for that restructuring. Emily, anything from the testing side?"

Emily smiled, her confidence evident. "Yes, Henry . I've identified a few scenarios where the new code isn't playing well with the existing test cases. We might need to update our test suite."

"Okay, that's crucial," Henry said, rubbing his chin thoughtfully. "Let's schedule a meeting to discuss the changes to the test suite. David, your thoughts?"

David, who had been quietly observing, joined the conversation. "I've been exploring some version control strategies that could help us avoid these conflicts in the future. Maybe we should implement a stricter branching model."

"Alright, let's have a separate session to deep dive into that," Henry responded, impressed by David's initiative. "Everyone, make sure to document your findings, and let's regroup in two days to discuss the progress."

As the meeting concluded and his team logged off, Henry leaned back in his chair, feeling a mix of satisfaction and lingering anxiety about Ava's school admission. Suddenly, his phone rang, breaking the brief moment of silence.

Glancing at the caller ID, he saw it was the admissions office for the prestigious Academy of Technology and Innovation. His heart rate quickened as he answered the call, a knot of anticipation tightening in his chest.

"Hello, Henry, this is Ms. Lee Carter from the Academy of Technology and Innovation. I'm calling to discuss your daughter's admission."

Henry felt a knot tighten in his stomach, his breath catching as he steadied himself. "Hello, Ms. Carter. What would you like to discuss?" he asked, his voice wavering slightly despite his efforts to remain calm.

"Well, first of all, let me say that we were very impressed with Ava's genetic profile. She has a rare combination of skills that would be an asset to our school," Ms. Carter began, her tone warm yet professional.

Henry's heart swelled with pride. He had always known that Ava was special. "Thank you," he managed, a small smile tugging at his lips.

"However," Ms. Carter continued, "we do have some concerns about her physical abilities. According to her genetic profile, she may struggle with certain physical tasks that are required for some of our programs."

Henry frowned, a sinking feeling replacing his initial joy. He hoped that her other skills would make up for it. "What does that mean for her admission?" he asked, his voice dropping.

"We'd like to schedule a meeting with you and your wife to discuss Ava's strengths and weaknesses in more detail. We'll also need to conduct some physical assessments to determine her abilities. After that, we'll be able to make a final decision about her admission."

Henry nodded, even though Ms. Carter couldn't see him. "Of course. When would be a good time for the meeting?" he asked, glancing at his calendar, the dates blurring as his mind raced.

"How about next Tuesday at 10 a.m.? We'll send you the details and the address of the school."

"Sounds good," Henry said, jotting down the appointment. "Thank you for letting us know."

"Thank you, Henry. We look forward to meeting with you and your wife," Ms. Carter replied, her voice steady.

Henry hung up the phone and sighed deeply, running a hand through his hair. He knew that Ava's admission wasn't guaranteed, but he was determined to do everything he could to help her succeed. The thought of the physical assessments gnawed at him, the uncertainty weighing heavily on his mind.

In the dystopian city of Aurorium, the government controlled the admission of children into specialized skills based on their genetic profiling. The process was complex and required multiple steps. Parents had to apply for admission into the skill-based program when their child was born, providing detailed information about the child's genetic makeup, including any identified strengths and weaknesses.

Henry glanced out the window, the towering skyscrapers of Aurorium casting long shadows in the midday sun. He thought about the rigorous review process that awaited Ava's application, carried out by a team of school officials who would determine whether she was a suitable candidate for the program. He knew the stakes were high.

He took a deep breath, resolving to support Ava through whatever challenges lay ahead. They would face this as a family, determined to ensure that Ava would have the best possible future in Aurorium's demanding society.

On the appointed Tuesday, Henry, Victoria and Ava left their home an hour earlier than necessary, the anticipation and nervous energy driving them to be overly punctual. They stepped out into the bright morning of Aurorium, the city's relentless hum a backdrop to their thoughts. The family car, a sleek, self-driving vehicle, awaited them at the curb. Henry loaded their bags into the trunk, his movements deliberate, trying to mask his anxiety.

As they settled into the car, Ava's eyes widened with curiosity. The dashboard lit up with a holographic map showing their route to the Academy of Technology and Innovation. The vehicle's AI greeted them with a calm, reassuring voice, "Good morning. We are on our way to the Academy. Estimated time of arrival: 9:00 AM."

Victoria looked at Ava, her face a mix of excitement and apprehension. "How are you feeling, sweetheart?" she asked, gently stroking Ava's hair. Ava's small hands fidgeting with the hem of her dress.

Henry glanced at the rearview mirror, catching Victoria's eye. They exchanged a look that spoke volumes—a mixture of hope, fear, and determination. "We'll be there with you every step of the way," Henry said, his voice firm but tender. "Just remember to do your best."

The car glided smoothly through the streets of Aurorium, the city's futuristic skyline reflecting off the windows. Towering skyscrapers, adorned with digital advertisements and glowing signs, loomed above them. Pedestrians moved briskly on the walkways, and drones buzzed overhead, delivering packages and monitoring traffic.

Inside the car, an uneasy silence settled. Henry and Victoria were both lost in their thoughts. Henry stared out the window, his mind replaying the countless conversations and preparations they had made for this day. *Is Ava ready? Have we done everything we can?* His heart ached with the weight of these questions.

Victoria, seated behind him, was similarly consumed by her own worries. What if the tests are too hard for her? What if she's not accepted? She looked at Ava, who was now gazing out the window, seemingly entranced by the passing scenery. Victoria reached over and held Ava's hand, offering a reassuring squeeze.

They arrived at the academy precisely one hour before their scheduled appointment. The self-driving car parked itself smoothly in a designated spot near the main entrance. Henry and Victoria stepped out first, taking in the sight of the academy once more. The complex was an impressive testament to human ingenuity and technological advancement, its glass walls gleaming in the sunlight.

Henry opened the door for Ava, helping her out of the car. As they walked towards the entrance, the enormity of the moment struck him again. This is it, he thought, his heart pounding. He glanced at Victoria, who gave him a reassuring nod. They both knew how much this opportunity meant for Ava.

The academy's entrance was bustling with activity, students and faculty moving with purpose. Holographic signs directed visitors to various parts of the campus, and the air was filled with a low hum of technology at work. Henry , Victoria and Ava walked through the main doors, the cool air of the interior a welcome contrast to the warmth outside.

They approached the reception desk, where an Humanoid assistant greeted them with a friendly smile. "Welcome to the Academy of Technology and Innovation. How may I assist you today?"

"We're here for our daughter's assessment," Henry replied, his voice steady despite the butterflies in his stomach. "Ava Parker ."

The AI's eyes flickered for a moment as it accessed the schedule. "Ah, yes. Ava Parker . Your appointment is at 10:00 AM. Please follow the illuminated path to the waiting area."

The floor lit up with a soft, guiding glow, leading them down a corridor lined with interactive displays showcasing the academy's achievements. As they walked, Henry and Victoria couldn't help but feel a mix of awe and nervousness.

They reached the waiting area, a sleek and modern space filled with comfortable seating and calming visuals projected on the walls. Henry checked the time—still an hour to go. He sat down beside Ava, who was swinging her legs nervously. Victoria took a seat on Ava's other side, placing a comforting arm around her.

"Remember, Ava," Victoria said softly, "this is just one step. Whatever happens, we're proud of you. Just be yourself and show them what you're capable of."

Henry took a deep breath, trying to calm his racing heart. He knew the next hour would be one of the longest they had ever experienced, filled with anticipation and hope for their daughter's future. Together, they waited, drawing strength from each other, ready to face whatever lay ahead.

As the family waited, the time seemed to stretch endlessly, each second a reminder of the impending assessment. At precisely 10:00 AM, an impeccably dressed woman approached them, her presence exuding confidence and professionalism.

"Mr. and Mrs. Parker, Ava," she greeted warmly. "I'm Lee Carter. It's a pleasure to meet you all. If you'll follow me, I'll give you a brief overview of the Academy before we proceed with Ava's assessments."

Henry and Victoria stood up, each offering a nervous but polite smile, while Ava clung tightly to Victoria's hand. They followed Ms. Carter down a sleek corridor, where the walls were lined with holographic displays showcasing various aspects of the academy.

Ms. Carter led them into a spacious, high-tech room. At the centre stood a humanoid robot, its design sleek and sophisticated, with an almost human like demeanour. The room darkened slightly, and the robot came to life, its eyes glowing softly.

"Good morning." the robot greeted in a calm, soothing voice. "My name is EDU-4, and I will be guiding you through the presentation about the Academy of Technology and Innovation."

With a subtle gesture from EDU-4, a series of holographic images sprang to life around them. The room was suddenly filled with three-dimensional projections of the academy's sprawling campus, its state-of-the-art facilities, and vibrant student life.

"Welcome to the Academy of Technology and Innovation," EDU-4 began, the holographic images shifting to show different aspects of the school. "Our institution is designed to nurture the unique genetic profiles of each student, offering specialized education tailored to their strengths and abilities."

Henry and Victoria watched in awe as the holograms displayed various classrooms, laboratories, and recreational areas. The futuristic architecture and cutting-edge technology were unlike anything they had ever seen.

"The academy is divided into four major streams," EDU-4 continued, the holograms now showing students engaged in various activities. "Engineering, Medical, Science, and Humanities. Each stream is meticulously designed to enhance the students' inherent skills and provide them with the best possible education."

The holograms zoomed in on each stream, showing students working with advanced robotics in Engineering, conducting intricate experiments in Medical and Science, and engaging in deep discussions in Humanities. The level of detail and innovation was staggering.

"Every student's journey begins with a comprehensive genetic profile analysis," EDU-4 explained. "This helps us understand their strengths and areas of potential development. Based on this profile, students are initially placed in the most suitable stream. However, we recognize that abilities and interests can evolve, so there are opportunities to transition between streams."

Henry glanced at Victoria, seeing the same mix of amazement and apprehension in her eyes that he felt. They both knew how much this meant for Ava.

"The selection process includes a series of tests," EDU-4 continued. "These tests are designed to assess both mental and physical abilities, ensuring that each student is placed in a stream that best matches their potential. The tests include cognitive assessments, problem-solving exercises, and physical evaluations tailored to each age group."

The holograms shifted to show students taking various tests, from intricate puzzle-solving to physical agility courses. Each student was accompanied by an AI tutor, offering guidance and support.

"We believe in a holistic approach to education," EDU-4 stated, its tone almost reverent. "Our goal is to create an environment where every student can thrive, developing not only their academic skills but also their physical and emotional well-being."

The final holograms displayed smiling students, engaged in group projects, athletic activities, and artistic endeavors. The academy appeared to be a place of limitless possibilities, where every child could find their path.

Ms. Carter stepped forward as the holographic presentation concluded. "As you can see, the Academy of Technology and Innovation is committed to providing an unparalleled educational experience. We understand that the selection process can be daunting, but please know that our goal is to find the best fit for each student, ensuring they have the opportunity to excel."

Henry took a deep breath, feeling a sense of hope and determination. "Thank you, Ms. Carter, and EDU-4. This has been incredibly informative."

Victoria nodded, her eyes shining with a mix of emotions. "Yes, thank you. We're excited for Ava to have this opportunity."

Ms. Carter smiled warmly. "That's wonderful to hear. Let's proceed with your assessments, and remember, we're here to support you every step of the way."

With a final reassuring glance at each other, Henry and Victoria followed Ms. Carter and EDU-4, ready to face the next step in their journey at the Academy of Technology and Innovation.

Henry, Victoria, and Ava followed Ms. Carter through the futuristic hallways of the Academy, the ambient lighting and sleek, modern design a stark contrast to the world outside. They arrived at a large, transparent door that slid open silently to reveal a spacious room filled with various high-tech equipment. The room was both clinical and welcoming, designed to put young children at ease while still serving its purpose for detailed assessments.

Ms. Carter turned to the family, her expression warm and reassuring. "This is where we will conduct Ava's assessments. We understand that this can be a bit overwhelming, but please know that our team is here to ensure Ava is comfortable and supported throughout the process."

Henry and Victoria exchanged a glance, both feeling a mix of anxiety and hope. Henry knelt down beside Ava, his eyes filled with encouragement. "You're going to do great, sweetheart. Just be yourself."

Ava, sensing the importance of the moment, nodded solemnly. Her tiny hands clutched her favorite stuffed animal, a source of comfort amid the unfamiliar surroundings.

A gentle-looking humanoid robot approached them, its design child friendly with soft edges and a calming presence. "Hello, Ava," the robot greeted with a smile. "My name is PAL, and I'll be helping you with your tests today. Are you ready to have some fun?"

Ava looked up at the robot, her initial apprehension fading slightly at the friendly tone. She nodded again, curiosity sparkling in her eyes.

The first part of the assessment was a cognitive test. PAL led Ava to a low table where a series of colorful, interactive puzzles were laid out. Each puzzle was designed to test different aspects of cognitive development, such as problem-solving skills, memory, and spatial awareness.

"Let's start with this one, Ava," PAL said, pointing to a puzzle with different shapes and holes. "Can you match the shapes to the right places?"

Ava sat down and began working on the puzzle, her tiny fingers moving with surprising dexterity. Henry and Victoria watched intently, their hearts swelling with pride and nerves. They knew Ava was smart, but seeing her engage with the puzzles so confidently filled them with both relief and hope.

Ms. Carter observed quietly from the side, her eyes reflecting a professional focus mixed with a genuine care for Ava's well-being. She noted Ava's quick thinking and determination, attributes that would serve her well in the academy.

After Ava successfully completed the cognitive puzzles, PAL guided her to the next section of the room where the physical assessments would take place. This area was equipped with soft mats, small obstacles, and various toys designed to assess motor skills and physical abilities.

"Now, Ava," PAL said gently, "we're going to play a game. Can you crawl through this tunnel and find the toy at the end?"

Ava's eyes widened with excitement at the prospect of a game. She glanced back at her parents, who smiled and nodded encouragingly. With a burst of energy, she crawled through the brightly colored tunnel, giggling as she reached the toy at the end.

Henry and Victoria's emotions were a whirlwind of pride and anxiety. They exchanged looks filled with silent support and mutual determination to help Ava succeed. They held hands, finding strength in each other as they watched their daughter navigate the challenges.

Ms. Carter stepped closer to Henry and Victoria, her voice low and reassuring. "Ava is doing wonderfully. These assessments are designed to be as engaging and non-stressful as possible. We're looking for her natural responses and abilities."

Henry nodded, his grip tightening on Victoria's hand. "Thank you, Ms. Carter. It means a lot to us to see Ava doing well."

The next test involved balance and coordination. PAL placed small, cushioned stepping stones on the floor and asked Ava to walk across them.

Ava wobbled a bit at first but soon found her balance, her face lighting up with concentration and determination.

As Ava completed the physical assessments, Henry and Victoria felt a deep sense of relief and pride. Their little girl had faced each challenge with resilience and enthusiasm. Ms. Carter observed silently, noting Ava's capabilities and potential.

When the assessments were finished, PAL led Ava back to her parents, who enveloped her in a tight, loving embrace. "You did amazing, Ava," Victoria whispered, her voice thick with emotion.

Ms. Carter smiled warmly at the family. "Ava has shown remarkable abilities today. We'll review the results and discuss the next steps with you shortly. Thank you for being here and supporting her."

Henry and Victoria nodded, their hearts full of hope and gratitude. As they left the assessment room, they felt a renewed sense of confidence in Ava's future at the Academy of Technology and Innovation, ready to face whatever lay ahead together as a family.

Henry, Victoria and Ava settled into the waiting room, a spacious area filled with soft, comfortable chairs and soothing colors designed to put families at ease. The room was quiet from the other parts of the academy. Despite the calming environment, tension was palpable in the air as they waited for the assessment results.

Henry paced back and forth, unable to sit still. His mind raced with thoughts of what the results might hold for Ava's future. Every now and then, he glanced at his watch, the minutes stretching into what felt like hours.

Victoria sat with Ava on her lap, gently stroking her hair. Ava, sensing the unease around her, clung to her stuffed animal and nestled closer to her mother. Victoria's face was a mix of worry and determination. She tried to maintain a calm exterior for Ava's sake, but inside, her heart was pounding.

Henry finally stopped pacing and took a seat next to Victoria, letting out a deep sigh. He leaned forward, resting his elbows on his knees and rubbing his temples.

"This waiting is torture," Henry muttered, his voice tinged with frustration.

Victoria looked at him, her eyes softening. "I know, but we have to stay positive. Ava did so well in the assessments. We need to trust that everything will work out."

Henry nodded, though the anxiety didn't leave his face. "I just keep thinking about all the what-ifs. What if she didn't perform well enough? What if they don't see how special she is?"

Victoria reached out and took his hand, squeezing it gently. "Henry , Ava is amazing. We saw how she handled those tests. She's smart, resilient, and full of potential. Whatever happens, we'll figure it out together."

Henry looked at Victoria, his eyes reflecting a mix of fear and hope. "You're right. I know you're right. It's just hard not to worry."

Victoria smiled faintly, brushing a strand of hair away from her face. "I worry too, but we have to believe in her. And in us. We've come this far, and we'll keep fighting for her."

Ava shifted on Victoria's lap, looking up at her parents with wide, curious eyes. Victoria kissed Ava's forehead and smiled.

Ava's face lit up with a smile, her earlier nervousness melting away. She hugged her stuffed animal tighter, comforted by her parents' words.

The door to the waiting room opened, and Ms. Carter walked in, holding a tablet. Her expression was warm and reassuring, though the air of professionalism remained.

"Thank you for your patience," Ms. Carter said as she approached them. "We've reviewed Ava's assessments, and I'd like to discuss the results with you."

Henry and Victoria stood up, their nerves returning in full force. They exchanged a glance, a silent message of mutual support passing between them. Holding Ava's hand, they followed Ms. Carter to a small, private office adjacent to the waiting room.

Ms. Carter entered the room, her expression more somber than before. She held the tablet close to her chest and took a deep breath before speaking.

"Mr. and Mrs. Parker ," she began, her voice gentle but firm, "I'm afraid I have some difficult news regarding Ava's assessment results."

Henry's heart sank, and he could feel his pulse quicken. He reached for Victoria's hand, squeezing it tightly. Victoria's face went pale, her eyes wide with worry.

Ms. Carter continued, "Ava performed exceptionally well on her cognitive assessments, showing remarkable problem-solving skills and a keen intellect. However, her physical assessment results were concerning. She struggled significantly with the physical tasks, and unfortunately, this is a critical aspect of our program."

Victoria's eyes filled with tears, and she instinctively pulled Ava closer to her. Ava, sensing her mother's distress, looked up with a puzzled expression.

Henry's jaw tightened, and he fought to keep his composure. "What does this mean for Ava's admission?" he asked, his voice strained.

Ms. Carter sighed softly, her eyes filled with sympathy. "Given the importance of physical abilities in our curriculum, we have to take these results into serious consideration. Unfortunately, we cannot offer Ava a place in the program at this time."

The room seemed to close in around them. Henry felt a crushing weight on his chest, his hopes shattered. He looked at Victoria, who was now openly crying, her face a mask of grief and disappointment. Ava, confused and concerned, reached up to wipe her mother's tears with her small hands.

Henry took a deep breath, his voice shaking as he spoke. "Thank you for letting us know, Ms. Carter," he said, though his words were tinged with bitterness. "We appreciate your honesty."

Ms. Carter nodded, her expression deeply empathetic. "I understand this is incredibly disappointing news. Please know that Ava's cognitive abilities are outstanding, and there may be other programs better suited to her strengths. We're happy to provide recommendations and support in finding the right fit for her."

Victoria looked at Ms. Carter, her eyes red and swollen. "We just want what's best for Ava," she said, her voice barely above a whisper. "It's hard to hear that she didn't meet the requirements."

Ms. Carter reached out and placed a comforting hand on Victoria's arm. "Ava has immense potential. This setback doesn't define her. It's just a matter of finding the right path for her unique talents."

Henry nodded, though his mind was still reeling from the news. "Thank you," he said again, his voice hollow. "We'll take some time to process this and figure out our next steps."

Ms. Carter gave them a compassionate smile. "If you need any assistance or have any questions, please don't hesitate to reach out. We wish Ava all the best in her future endeavors."

As they left the office, Henry and Victoria walked in silence, each lost in their thoughts. Ava, sensing the heaviness in the air, clung to her mother's hand, her earlier cheerfulness replaced with uncertainty.

Once they were outside the academy, Henry pulled Victoria into a tight embrace, trying to offer some comfort even as his own heart ached. "We'll find another way," he whispered, his voice breaking. "Ava will thrive, I know she will. We'll do whatever it takes."

Together, they walked towards the car, determined to face the challenges ahead as a family, their love for Ava giving them the strength to move forward.

Henry and Victoria, determined to find the right place for Ava, began their journey through the elite schools of Aurorium with renewed determination. Each rejection was a blow, but their resolve only grew stronger.

The Second Rejection

The second school they approached was the prestigious Aurora Academy, known for its emphasis on holistic development and state-of-the-art facilities. They were hopeful, remembering stories of children with diverse talents flourishing in its nurturing environment.

However, as they sat in the opulent waiting room, with its glass walls offering panoramic views of the city, Henry and Victoria couldn't help but feel a sense of dread. The principal, a stern woman with sharp eyes, greeted them with a practiced smile. After reviewing Ava's application and assessment results, she sighed, her expression shifting to one of regret. "I'm afraid Ava's physical assessment scores fall below our required threshold," she said, her tone polite but firm. "While her cognitive abilities are remarkable, our programs demand a balance of both mental and physical prowess. I'm sorry, but we cannot offer her a place at Aurora Academy."

The Third Rejection

Undeterred, Henry and Victoria turned to the Solaris Institute, renowned for its cutting-edge technology and individualized learning paths. The institute's sleek, futuristic building shimmered under the city lights as they approached. Inside, holographic displays showcased student achievements and innovative projects.

They met with Dr. Mitchell, the admissions director, in a room filled with interactive screens and AI assistants. He reviewed Ava's file, nodding thoughtfully.

"Ava's intellectual potential is impressive," he began, but Henry and Victoria braced for the inevitable 'however.' "However, our curriculum is physically demanding. The physical assessments are critical in determining a student's ability to keep up with our rigorous programs. I'm afraid Ava does not meet the physical criteria. We must prioritize the overall well being and success of our students."

The Fourth Rejection

Next, they visited the Lumina School for Gifted Children, a beacon of hope for parents across Aurorium. The school's reputation for nurturing prodigies gave them a glimmer of optimism. The headmaster, Mr. Gaines, welcomed them warmly, his office decorated with awards and accolades.

After discussing Ava's talents and aspirations, Mr. Gaines leaned back in his chair, a look of sympathy on his face. "Ava is undoubtedly gifted," he said, "but our program's physical demands are non-negotiable. We strive to ensure that all our students can fully participate in every aspect of our curriculum. Unfortunately, Ava's physical assessment results indicate she would struggle with our requirements. I wish we could make an exception, but it's simply not feasible."

The Fifth Rejection

Their final attempt was at the Zenith Academy, a school celebrated for its comprehensive approach to education, blending academics with physical training. As they entered the grand halls lined with trophies and digital art displays, Henry and Victoria felt a mix of hope and fear.

The admissions officer, Ms. Rivera, reviewed Ava's application meticulously. She looked up, her eyes filled with regret. "Ava's intellectual capabilities are exceptional," she acknowledged. "But our programs integrate physical activities deeply into the learning process. Her physical assessment scores indicate she would have significant difficulty keeping pace. I'm truly sorry, but we cannot accept her into Zenith Academy."

The Aftermath

Each rejection left Henry and Victoria more heartbroken and frustrated. They sat in their car after the last meeting, the weight of their efforts crashing down on them. Victoria stared out the window, her eyes filled with unshed tears. "Why does it always come down to her physical abilities?" she whispered, her voice trembling with anguish.

Henry took her hand, squeezing it gently. "I don't know," he admitted, his voice thick with emotion. "But we can't give up. There has to be a place where Ava's strengths are enough."

As they drove home, the city lights blurred into a haze, reflecting their muddled emotions. Henry and Victoria resolved to keep searching, believing that somewhere in Aurorium, there was a school that would recognize and nurture Ava's unique talents. Despite the repeated rejections, their love for Ava and their faith in her potential kept them moving forward, one hopeful step at a time.

It was late evening. In the dimly lit living room, Henry sank into the armchair, weariness etched across his face. Victoria, his wife, sat beside him, holding Ava. After a long day, their daughter slept peacefully in her mother's arms, unaware of the struggles her parents faced. Victoria's eyes reflected the same concern that shadowed Henry 's mind.

Henry sighed heavily, breaking the heavy silence. "It's been weeks, Victoria, and we still can't secure a spot for Ava in any of those schools."

Victoria nodded, her voice tinged with frustration. "It's frustrating. We've been dreaming of providing her with opportunities we never had."

Henry ran a hand through his hair, his expression pained. "I don't want her to struggle like we did. She's smart, Victoria, she deserves a chance at a better future."

Victoria placed a comforting hand on Henry 's shoulder, her touch gentle yet resolute. "We've done everything we can, contacted every school, filled out countless forms, and still, it feels like we're hitting a wall."

Henry's gaze softened as he looked at Ava in Victoria's arms. "She's such a bright kid. She should be getting the best education, not being confined by our limitations."

Victoria rested her head on Henry 's shoulder, her voice a quiet murmur of determination. "We can't give up, Henry . We'll keep trying. We'll find a way for Ava."

As they shared this emotional conversation, the determination in their eyes spoke of a shared commitment to ensuring a better future for Ava, no matter the obstacles in their way. In the dim light, they held onto each other and their resolve, drawing strength from their love and the promise of a brighter tomorrow for their daughter.

Feeling dejected and frustrated, Henry and Victoria decided to visit the Ministry of Education to complain about the injustice they were facing. As they approached the grand, imposing building, they noticed the somber expressions on the faces of those exiting. Parents, their faces etched with worry and sadness, clutched the hands of their children. Individuals of all ages and backgrounds departed with disappointment deeply etched into their features, a sign that the system had failed yet another group of hopefuls. The air was thick with a shared sense of defeat, as if the building itself had drained the last vestiges of hope from everyone who walked through its doors.

Finally, it was their turn to speak to the officer. They were led into a drab office where a government official, his demeanor cool and detached, sat behind a cluttered desk. The room was stark and unwelcoming, with grey walls and fluorescent lights that cast a harsh glow on the officer's indifferent face. Without looking up from his computer, he gestured lazily towards the chairs in front of his desk.

"Have a seat," he mumbled, his voice devoid of any warmth or welcome.

Henry and Victoria exchanged a quick glance before sitting down. Henry clutched a file filled with paperwork, a tangible representation of their struggle. He began explaining their situation, his voice steady but laced with frustration.

"Thank you for seeing us. We've been trying to get our daughter, Ava, into a good school for months now. We've contacted every school we can think of, filled out countless forms, and still, no luck. She's an exceptionally bright child, and we believe she deserves the best education possible."

The officer continued to type on his computer, his eyes rarely meeting Henry's. Occasionally, he glanced at the screen, more interested in the flickering lines of text than in the desperate plea being made in front of him.

When Henry finished, the officer finally looked up, his expression one of practiced sympathy that didn't reach his eyes. "I'm sorry, but we can't do anything for you," he said, his tone flat and dismissive. "The schools have their own criteria for admissions, and we can't force them to accept your daughter."

Victoria, her face a mix of desperation and determination, leaned forward, her voice trembling with emotion. "But isn't education a basic human right? Shouldn't every child have equal opportunity to learn and grow?"

The officer sighed, clearly exasperated. "Listen," he began, his voice dripping with condescension, "I understand your frustration, but this is the way things are. You could try in other districts, but they are not as good as the ones you are looking for. However, I can assure you that admission to some school is guaranteed, even if it's not the one you prefer."

His words felt hollow, his tone suggesting that their plea was just another routine complaint in a long list of grievances he had to handle daily. He leaned back in his chair, his body language screaming disinterest, as if he couldn't wait for this interaction to be over so he could return to his mundane tasks.

Henry and Victoria exchanged a glance, feeling a mix of anger and helplessness. The officer's dismissive attitude was a stark reminder of the bureaucratic wall they were up against. Henry stood up, his jaw clenched tightly with suppressed emotion. "Thank you for your time," he said, his voice strained and barely concealing his frustration. He took Victoria's hand, feeling the warmth and strength in her grip, and they walked out of the office together, their steps heavy with the weight of disappointment.

As they exited the Ministry of Education, the weight of hopelessness pressed down on them. The faces of those they passed mirrored their own despair. Parents walked out holding their children close, their eyes reflecting a mixture of sorrow and resignation. They had hoped for a glimmer of justice, for someone to see their plight and help them. Instead, they were met with bureaucratic indifference and an unyielding system.

Despite their despair, a flicker of determination remained in Henry and Victoria. They would continue to fight for Ava's future, no matter how many walls they had to break down. The officer's indifference had only strengthened their resolve. As they left the building, the cool evening air did little to lift their spirits, but it was a reminder that they had each other, and together, they would find a way.

The next day, seeking solace and counsel, Henry found himself at a coffee shop where he rendezvoused with his friend Jack. The aroma of freshly ground beans permeated the air as they settled into their chairs, each carrying a cup in hand. Henry gazed into his coffee, his mind preoccupied with the weight of a recent struggle.

Jack leaned forward, concern etched on his face. "Come on, Henry. What's eating you up?" Henry hesitated for a moment, staring into the swirling patterns in his coffee. Finally, he began to share his recent challenge. "It's just not fair, Jack," he said. "How can a machine determine my daughter's future? Ava was rejected from the Science stream solely based on her average motor skills, despite having a great cognition assessment score. It's just not right."

Jack listened intently, nodding his head in agreement. "I understand your frustration, Henry," he said. "But unfortunately, this is the world we live in now. AI is becoming increasingly important in decision-making, and it's only going to get more prevalent in the future."

Jack sighed, leaning back in his chair. "You know, Henry, it's not just about Ava. The government is always favoring the rich and influential people to get admission into the best schools. Even if they don't meet the eligibility criteria, they manage to get their way in."

Henry looked up sharply. "What do you mean? Are you saying that Ava didn't get admission because we are not influential or rich?"

"Exactly," Jack replied. "Look at the other schools you tried to get her into. They were all full, right? But do you know who they managed to get in? The children of those politicians and businessmen who didn't even meet the requirements. They just used their power and influence to get their children admitted."

Henry clenched his fist around his coffee cup. "That's not fair. Everyone should have equal opportunities. It's not just about being rich or influential. It's about talent and hard work."

"I completely agree with you, Henry," Jack said earnestly. "But unfortunately, that's not the case in our society. We need to do something about it. We need to fight for our rights and stand up against this injustice."

Henry felt a surge of determination. "You're right, Jack. We can't just sit back and let this happen. We need to take action and make our voices heard. Our children deserve the same opportunities as everyone else."

As they finished their conversation, Henry felt more determined than ever to fight for his daughter's right to education and equality.

2

The Trap

Henry sat before his computer, his fingers hammering the keyboard with a relentless urgency. The bluish glow of the screen etched determination onto his furrowed brow as he painstakingly constructed a digital lifeline—a platform for those crushed beneath the weight of bias in the school admission system. Every keystroke was a cry for justice, fueled by the bitter memories of his own family's battle.

The journey he and Victoria endured to secure a decent school for their daughter, Ava, played like a haunting reel in his mind. Each rejection letter, every dismissive conversation, and the helpless frustration etched on Ava's face ignited a fire within him—a fire that now blazed into action.

Pouring his story onto the digital canvas, Henry invited others to share theirs, a call to arms for every parent silenced by despair. The response was overwhelming. Like moths to a flame, parents flocked to his social media page, their narratives flooding in, each one more heart-wrenching than the last. The platform became a resounding echo chamber of pain and fury—a testament to a broken system.

With every story, Henry's resolve solidified. The tide of voices united him in an unwavering mission: to fight for a future where no child was denied their chance at education. He rallied the disheartened into a movement, organizing protests despite the looming shadow of government pushback.

Weeks of sleepless nights and meticulous planning culminated in a monumental moment—a peaceful demonstration outside the Education Minister's office. A vibrant sea of parents and activists stretched out, their faces determined, their collective voice demanding justice.

The air vibrated with chants, each one piercing through the oppressive silence of apathy. As police lines closed in, urging the crowd to disperse, the tension thickened. Suddenly, the heavy doors of the office swung open, and out stepped Mr. Smith, the Education Minister, his face a mask of forced composure.

"Please, I urge you all to listen," Mr. Smith began, his voice teetering between diplomacy and defensiveness. "I understand your concerns, but this chaos will not lead to solutions."

Henry stepped forward, his figure commanding attention. His voice, clear and resonant, cut through the murmurs like a blade.

"Minister, we've waited. We've hoped. And we've been ignored," Henry declared, his tone unwavering. "Today, we demand not words, but actions. Justice for our children can no longer be delayed."

A hushed stillness enveloped the crowd as Henry climbed a makeshift podium. All eyes fixed on him, the weight of their shared struggles resting on his shoulders. The air hung heavy with anticipation, and in that moment, Henry knew: this wasn't just his fight anymore—it was a fight for every child's future.

Henry: (voice impassioned) "We are here, not as agitators, but as advocates for justice. Our children face a biased system that privileges the few and marginalizes the deserving. This isn't merely a protest; it's a plea for fairness, for an educational system that upholds the promise of equal opportunity."

The crowd erupted in supportive cheers, their resolve mirrored in their loud affirmations.

Mr. Smith: (conciliatory) "I hear your concerns. There are proper channels to address these issues. Let's work together, not as adversaries but as partners in reform."

Henry: (steadfast) "Minister, those channels have failed us. We need action, tangible changes, not just dialogue."

The stand-off continued, a palpable clash of desperation and bureaucratic caution.

Mr. Smith, perhaps touched by the palpable sincerity in Henry's plea, softened slightly.

Mr. Smith : "Alright, I promise to review the admissions process. Give us a chance to rectify these wrongs."

As Minister Smith 's words permeated the charged air, the crowd that had amassed with banners of defiance and voices of protest began to transition from fervent clamor to a more subdued murmur. Henry, standing firm at the podium, cast a sweeping gaze over the assembly—a mosaic of determined faces, each painted with the streaks of struggle and hope.

The minister's promise, while met initially with skepticism, slowly seeped into the collective consciousness of the gathered crowd. His assurance to revisit and revise the admission process was a beam of potential progress in their shadowed fight. Parents exchanged looks of cautious optimism, their earlier chants softening into conversations about what had just transpired.

Henry stepped down from the podium, his presence still commanding attention as he moved among the protestors. He offered nods of appreciation and clasped hands with many, his expressions silently conveying a promise not to let their efforts go in vain.

Gradually, the signs that had arched towards the sky began to lower, and the group started to disperse. Small clusters formed, discussing the event's outcome and the minister's words, dissecting every possible implication.

The atmosphere, though still simmering with a residual urgency, was now tinged with a thread of hope.

As the crowd thinned, the space in front of the minister's office, which had been a tableau of civic engagement, began to clear, leaving behind only the echoes of their chants. The police, their earlier sternness replaced by relief, slowly retreated, their presence no longer necessary.

Henry lingered for a moment, surveying the area, ensuring everyone departed safely and without incident. His heart was heavy yet hopeful; the protest might have ended, but the campaign for justice had gained a new momentum.

With a deep breath, he turned and walked towards the parking lot where his car was stationed. The gravel crunched under his feet, a stark contrast to the earlier vibrancy of human voices. As he approached his car, a slight figure detached itself from the shadows of the nearby buildings—a government official, recognizable by the emblem pinned neatly on his jacket.

Henry, initially startled, watched as the man approached with a brisk pace, his face etched with the urgency of his message.

"Mr. Henry Parker?" the official called out, stopping a few feet away, his demeanor respectful yet insistent.

Henry paused, his hand on the car door. "Yes, that's me. Is there something I can help you with?"

The official, smoothing down his jacket, nodded. "I come with a message from the Education Minister, Mr.Smith. He was quite impressed with your articulation of the issues today and would like to discuss further how you can contribute to the reform efforts. He's requesting your presence at his office tomorrow morning."

Henry's eyebrows rose in surprise, mixed with a flicker of suspicion. The rapid invitation from the minister was unexpected, yet it spoke volumes about the impact of their demonstration.

"Thank you," Henry replied, his voice steady. "Tell the minister I appreciate the invitation and I will be there. It's crucial we keep this momentum going."

"Absolutely, Mr. Parker ," the official said, offering a small, professional smile. "We look forward to your insights. I'll let the minister know of your acceptance."

As the official turned to leave, Henry slid into his car, the weight of the day's events pressing down on him. He started the engine, the purr of the car a comforting sound in the cool evening air. As he drove away, his mind was already racing with strategies and plans. Tomorrow's meeting wasn't just a courtesy call—it was a pivotal opportunity to steer the course of educational reform.

Behind him, the government building stood silent, a witness to the day's plea for justice, now awaiting the seeds of change that had been sown on its steps.

The next day the office of Education Minister Mr. Smith was steeped in quietude when Henry Parker entered, the muffled sounds of the bustling city outside hardly permeating its thick, ornate walls. The room, a blend of old-world charm and modern sophistication, featured a massive oak desk littered with papers and digital displays showing various educational metrics. Along one wall, a series of screens displayed real-time data from the controversial AI-driven admissions system—a testament to modern technology's role in education.

"Henry, I'm glad you could make it," Mr. Smith began, his voice carrying a mix of cordiality and solemnity as he motioned Henry to sit across from him. He sat down, folding his hands on the desk, his gaze earnest.

Henry nodded, his expression taut with a blend of anticipation and skepticism. "Thank you, Minister. I understand we're here to discuss something significant?"

"Yes, indeed," Mr. Smith replied, leaning back slightly. "Our education system is at a crucial juncture. We've faced numerous challenges—corruption, inefficiencies... and now, potential flaws in our AI admissions system. It's our duty to address these issues head-on."

Henry 's eyebrows knitted together, his earlier suspicions now finding a voice. "When you say challenges, are we talking about the same AI system that's supposed to democratize education? Because from what I've seen, it seems to be doing quite the opposite."

Mr. Smith 's expression . "That's exactly what we need to discuss, Henry. You've been quite vocal and effective as a citizen advocate. I believe your insights could be invaluable to our Special Task Force aimed at rectifying these issues."

Henry shifted uncomfortably, the weight of the proposition dawning on him. "What role do you envision for me in this task force, Mr. Smith?"

"As a key member, Henry. You'll collaborate with experts to scrutinize and overhaul the system. We need someone who isn't afraid to challenge the status quo—someone who genuinely cares."

Henry paused, his mind racing. This was the opportunity to effect change he had been hoping for, yet the magnitude of the task was daunting.

"I won't lie, Minister. I'm hesitant. It's a massive responsibility. But... if it means we can fix this, ensure every child gets a fair shot—then I'm in."

Mr. Smith smiled, genuinely with gratitude. "That's all I can ask for."

In the confines of a small, cluttered office space, Henry and his team huddled over systems and stacks of documents. The room was a symphony of tapping keyboards and low murmurs, a testament to the intense focus that gripped them as they delved into the labyrinthine code of the AI algorithm responsible for school admissions. The task at hand was monumental—Henry was determined to uncover the biases that had unjustly skewed the system in favor of the privileged.

Henry, with a commanding yet empathetic presence, orchestrated the efforts, delegating tasks with precision. "Anna, focus on the section where socio-economic data is being factored into skill assessments. Look for any hidden weightings," he instructed, handing over a series of highlighted printouts. Anna nodded, her determination evident as she immersed herself in the code.

"Ravi," Henry continued, turning to another member, "cross-reference these outputs with real admission records. We need concrete evidence of discrepancies—any mismatched patterns that align with wealth indicators."

Ravi adjusted his glasses, eyes sharp with concentration, and began correlating the data sets. Meanwhile, Henry himself tackled the core algorithms, his fingers flying over the keyboard as he dissected each line with meticulous scrutiny.

Days melted into nights as the team pushed through fatigue, driven by a shared sense of purpose. Their relentless pursuit gradually unearthed troubling patterns: the algorithm subtly favored students from affluent backgrounds, assigning them higher skill assessment scores under the guise of potential. It was a digital facade, seemingly neutral yet insidiously discriminatory.

As the picture became clearer, Henry compiled the evidence into a comprehensive report. He highlighted instances where the system unjustly penalized students like Ava, penalizing them for factors beyond their control. With charts, code snippets, and statistical analyses, the document painted a stark picture of inequality woven into the AI's logic.

With the evidence in hand, Henry prepared for his meeting with Minister Smith. This was more than just a report—it was a call to action, a demand for justice and reform. The truth was out in the open, and Henry was ready to confront the powers that be, armed with undeniable proof of a system that had failed its most vulnerable members.

Realizing the importance of his findings, Henry had approached the Minister's personal assistant, Ms. Melissa, a meticulous woman known for her strict gatekeeping of the Minister's schedule.

"Ms. Melissa," Henry had started, his tone respectful yet firm, "I need to discuss an urgent matter regarding the AI admissions system with Minister Smith. It's of utmost importance and could have wide-reaching implications."

Ms. Melissa, who was used to the usual requests for the Minister's time, looked up from her desk, peering at Henry over her glasses. "Mr. HenryParker, do you have an appointment?" she asked in neutral voice.

"I don't, but I assure you, this cannot wait. It's about a critical flaw in the system that unfairly affects thousands of students. I've conducted a thorough analysis," Henry had replied holding the tab (with all findings).

Noting the seriousness in his voice and the documentation in his hands, Ms. Melissa had paused, assessing the situation. "Alright, Mr. Henry. I

understand the urgency. Let me see what I can do. Please take a seat, and I'll inform the Minister about your request."

"Thank you, Ms. Melissa. I appreciate your help," Henry said, his tone relieved yet underscored by the anxiety of the impending wait.

Every tick of the clock amplified Henry's eagerness to step in and lay out the evidence he had gathered. His body mirrored this urgency, a stark contrast to the usual tranquility of the administrative corridor. This was a moment he had prepared for, not just as a professional but as a citizen deeply committed to fairness and integrity in education. His readiness was palpable, his resolve as firm as the documents in his hand.

After what seemed like an interminable wait, Ms. Melissa emerged from the Minister's office with a composed expression, her steps measured and precise. As she approached Henry, who was now seated on one of the plush chairs lining the corridor, his body tensed in anticipation, his eyes tracking her every movement.

"Mr. Henry Parker," Ms. Melissa began, her voice clear and professional, "Minister Smith will see you now. He's ready to discuss the concerns you've raised."

Henry immediately stood up, his movements quick and slightly abrupt, a clear indication of his eagerness. "Thank you, Ms. Melissa he replied, his voice steady but carrying an undertone of urgency.

She nodded, giving him a small, encouraging smile. "Right this way," she said, leading him towards the door. As they approached, she reached out and gently tapped on the door, which swung open silently.

"Minister Smith, Mr. Henry Parker is here to see you regarding the AI admissions system," Ms. Melissa announced as she gestured for Henry to enter.

"Thank you, Ms. Melissa the Minister's voice echoed from within, warm yet authoritative. "Please, come in, Henry."

As Henry stepped past the threshold, Ms. Melissa gave him a final nod, a silent gesture of goodwill, before she quietly closed the door behind him, leaving him to navigate the waters of high-stakes discussion that awaited him inside.

"Minister Smith," Henry began, his voice firm despite the fluttering in his stomach, "thank you for meeting me today. I've uncovered something in our AI admissions system that requires immediate attention."

He leaned forward, placing the sleek tablet on the desk so that it faced the Minister. His finger swiped through screens filled with graphs and numbers, each swipe revealing another layer of the issue at hand.

"As you can see here," Henry continued, pointing to a particularly striking bar graph, "the algorithm assigns weight to various parameters when assessing a student's application. However, I've discovered a disturbing bias in how socio-economic factors are weighted."

Minister Smith 's eyes narrowed slightly, his interest piqued as he leaned forward to get a better view of the data displayed. "Go on," he prompted, his voice smooth yet edged with a hint of skepticism.

Henry tapped on another chart, which showed a clear discrepancy in acceptance rates. "This scatter plot represents student scores versus acceptance outcomes. You'll notice a trend where students from higher socio-economic backgrounds have a disproportionately higher acceptance rate, even with similar academic scores to their less affluent peers."

The Minister stroked his chin, his expression unreadable. "Interesting," he murmured. "And how certain are you of these findings, Mr. Henry?"

"Very certain, sir," Henry replied, his confidence bolstered by the hours of analysis he had conducted. "I've run multiple tests, recalibrating the algorithm without the socio-economic factor, and the bias disappears."

Minister Smith tapped a finger against his lips, a gesture that seemed thoughtful yet somehow calculated. "This is a serious allegation, Henry. It implies that our system isn't just flawed—it's fundamentally unfair."

"Exactly, sir," Henry agreed, his eyes locked on the Minister's. "It's critical that we address this. We can't claim to provide equal educational opportunities while a flaw like this exists."

Minister Smith paused, his gaze drifting back to the tablet before returning to Henry. His next words came slowly, laced with a hint of a smile that didn't quite reach his eyes. "You've done commendable work uncovering this, Henry. It takes courage to bring such matters to light."

Henry felt a stir of hope, sensing an ally in his quest for justice. "Thank you, Minister. I believe with some adjustments, we can rectify this issue and truly level the playing field for all applicants."

The Minister stood up, his presence dominating the room. "Indeed, we will look into it. But let's keep this between us for now. We wouldn't want to cause unnecessary panic or give rise to unwarranted criticism before we have a solution in place."

Henry nodded, understanding the political delicacy of the situation, yet he couldn't shake off a faint, unsettling feeling that the Minister's agreeable demeanor masked deeper, perhaps not so benevolent intentions.

As the twilight shadows deepened, Henry's tranquil evening with his family was shattered by the pounding on the door. Before Victoria could fully turn the handle, officers in dark uniforms stormed inside, their movements brisk and forceful. As the door swung open, one of the officers, a burly man with a stern face, grabbed Henry from behind, pinning his arms in a vice-like grip. Ava, witnessing the sudden intrusion, retreated behind her mother, her cries piercing the tense air.

"Henry Parker , you're under arrest for unauthorized access to government computer systems," the officer announced loudly, his voice echoing in the small living room. Henry's heart sank; the accusation seemed ludicrous, a nightmare unfolding in real-time.

Victoria, eyes wide with fear and confusion, clutched Ava closer. "What's happening, Henry? What are they talking about?" she stammered, struggling to shield their daughter from the distressing scene.

Henry met her gaze, his expression a mix of resolve and pain. "Victoria, listen to me," he urged, his voice steady despite the chaos, "I haven't done anything wrong. This is a misunderstanding, and I'll sort it out." He tried to sound confident, but his voice betrayed the worry gnawing at him. The officer tightened his grip, steering Henry towards the door. "We have evidence of your intrusion into protected files. You'll have the chance to explain at the station," he stated flatly, devoid of sympathy.

As they led him away, Henry's reassurances lingered in the air, a thin thread of hope for Victoria to grasp. Meanwhile, Ava's cries faded into a heart-wrenching sob, marking the harsh close of what had started as an ordinary evening.

3

The Discriminating Society

In the quiet haze of an early Saturday morning, Victoria, accompanied by her young daughter Ava, pushed a cart through the automatic sliding doors of the local grocery store. The store, once a place of mundane routine, now harbored an air of surveillance that was palpable.

As they entered, a small humanoid robot, sleek and silvery, detached itself from its charging dock and began to tail them discreetly. Its eyes, bright with artificial intelligence, kept a vigilant watch on Victoria and Ava as they moved through the aisles. Victoria felt a chill down her spine, but she forced a smile for Ava, who looked curiously at the robot following them.

"Mama, why is it following us?" Ava asked, her voice low and uneasy.

Victoria squeezed her daughter's hand, "It's just making sure we find everything we need, sweetie," she replied, though her heart sank with the weight of knowing the real reason — their low social score.

They continued shopping, picking up necessities, but the usual ease of their grocery ritual was marred by the robot's persistent shadow. At the checkout, Victoria placed their items on the conveyor belt, her eyes avoiding the screens that usually displayed personalized discounts. She knew they wouldn't be seeing any discounts today.

As the cashier, a young man with a polite yet distant demeanor, scanned their items, Victoria mustered the courage to address the elephant in the room.

"Excuse me," she began, her voice steady despite the fluttering in her chest, "I noticed we didn't receive any discounts today. Is there a problem with my account?"

The cashier glanced at the screen, then back at Victoria with an expression that tread a fine line between professional and pitying. "I'm sorry, ma'am," he said, the words almost mechanical. "Discounts are applied based on social score thresholds. Unfortunately, your current score doesn't qualify for today's promotions."

Victoria nodded, a tight smile concealing the sting of the words. "I see," she replied, her voice calm though her mind raced with indignation. "And the robot? Does it also follow everyone around?"

"That's a new store policy for... certain scores," the cashier responded awkwardly, his eyes flicking to the humanoid that stood a respectful distance away.

Victoria drew a deep breath, her hand finding Ava's shoulder. "Thank you for explaining," she said, her tone laced with a hint of defiance. "Come on, Ava, let's go home."

They walked out into the sunlight, the door sliding shut behind them, leaving the watching eyes of the robot behind. In the safety of their shared understanding, they found a small, defiant spark of resilience.

Yet, the decay was not confined to physical spaces—it seeped into the very fabric of human connections. Acquaintances, once friends, recalibrated their loyalties, distancing themselves from Victoria and Henry to protect their own numerical worth. The social score—a singular, oppressive figure—loomed large, reshaping the dynamics of relationships and community bonds.

In this brave new world carved by algorithms, societal divisions were stark. Victoria and Henry, once integral threads in their community's weave, now navigated a fragmented landscape where their value was distilled to a mere number. This number, arbitrarily assigned, dictated their movements, their interactions, and the solidarity of those around them.

Amid the sterile glow of office fluorescents, Victoria, seated at her desk, hammered away at her tasks, her concentration punctuated by the drone of ambient office sounds. Christy, her cubicle neighbor, approached with a blend of concern and curiosity.

Christy: (*whispering*) Hey, Victoria. Did you catch wind of last night's gathering?

Victoria: (*looking up, feigning ignorance*) What gathering? Christy: (*hesitantly*) The surprise party in the breakroom... for Lisa. Victoria: (with feigned nonchalance) Oh, really? Must've missed that memo.

Christy: (*lowering her voice*) Victoria, I know they didn't invite you... I overheard Lisa mention your social score.

Victoria: (*with a wry smile*) Oh, right. The "social score." Because that's what really matters, isn't it?

Christy: (*apologetic*) I'm sorry, Victoria. It's absurd, I know. But some are just too scared of their scores dropping by association.

Victoria: (*sarcastically*) Great, so I'm the office outcast now?

Christy: (*softly*) Not to everyone. Just a few who are overly cautious about those numbers.

Victoria: (*sighing and leaning back*) I just focus on my work and keep to myself. Never thought I'd be bothered about missing a party.

Christy: (*supportive*) It's their loss, Victoria. You're a fantastic colleague and friend.

Victoria: (*smiling genuinely*) Thanks, Christy. Let's just get back to work. At least my job doesn't judge me based on some arbitrary number.

As Victoria resumed her tasks, the air in the office seemed to thicken with a palpable sense of injustice. The stark disparity between professional competence and social scores overshadowed what should have been a simple celebration of a colleague's birthday.

As Henry's arrest threatened the possibility of Ava's admission to school, Victoria took on the sole responsibility of raising their daughter. Haunted by the discrimination Ava faced due to her socio-economic status, Victoria chose to homeschool her, committed to providing a diverse and enriching education.

Despite the daunting challenges, Victoria was resolute. She spent hours researching various subjects, striving to devise creative and engaging lessons for Ava. Over time, Ava flourished, her academic prowess and innate curiosity about the world blossoming under her mother's guidance. Meanwhile, Henry's days blurred into one another in the stark confines of his cell, each day marked by the slow tick towards his impending trial.

The prison visiting room, cold and sterile, echoed with the subdued voices of other visitors and inmates, a stark backdrop for the emotional reunion of a fractured family. Henry, usually composed, felt his heart tighten as he saw Victoria walking towards him, their daughter Ava in tow. The little girl, now taller and more curious than he remembered, clung to her mother's hand with a shy smile.

As they approached, Henry rose unsteadily to his feet, his eyes never leaving the faces of his wife and daughter. The guard allowed them a rare privilege—a moment of gentle physical contact. Victoria and Ava extended their hands through the small opening of the partition. Henry's hands, trembling, reached out, touching their hands. His skin was cold, the warmth of their touch a stark contrast.

Victoria: (*voice quivering*) Henry, Today is Ava birthday. She wanted to see you. She missed you so much.

Henry: (*his voice breaking as he looked at Ava*) Hey, pumpkin. Look how big you've gotten! How old are you ?

Ava: I'm 4. Daddy, when are you coming home?

The simplicity of her question, laden with innocence and hope, shattered the last of Henry's composure. Tears streamed down his cheeks as he squeezed their hands gently.

Henry: (*choking up*) I'm trying, my love. I'm trying so hard. We'll be together soon, I promise.

Victoria: (*tears streaming down her face*) We're fighting for you, Henry. Every day, we're out there, telling your story, making sure they know you're innocent.

Henry nodded, his eyes locked on Ava, who was trying so hard to be brave in the face of confusing adult fears.

Henry: Ava, my brave girl, I want you to keep learning, keep exploring everything. Mommy is doing a great job, isn't she?

Ava: (*nodding*)

Victoria: (*softly, to Henry*) She asks about you every night.

The poignant moment stretched on, the three of them connected by touch, each comforted yet pained by the closeness. Henry, feeling the weight of his situation more acutely than ever, spoke again, his voice steadier but heavy with emotion.

Henry: (*firmly, as he looked from Victoria to Ava*) "Listen, both of you are my strength. No matter what happens, remember that I love you more than anything. Keep looking out for each other. Victoria, promise me you'll stay strong for Ava."

Victoria: (*nodding, resolute*) I promise, Henry. We won't give up. Not ever.

As the guards signalled that the time was up, Henry reluctantly let go of their hands. The physical separation felt abrupt, the warmth lingering on his fingertips a bittersweet reminder of what he was fighting to return to. Ava waved, a brave little smile on her face, while Victoria blew him a kiss, her eyes speaking volumes of love and determination. Henry sat back down, watching them leave, the echo of their love and courage fuelling his resolve to keep fighting, to return home to them, no matter what.

4

The Injustice

On a fine morning, a protest was unfolding in front of the Education Ministry building. A tall figure, clad in an overcoat, navigated through the passionate crowd, where voices clamored and placards waved in the air, creating a tense atmosphere charged with fervor. They were demanding justice for Henry Parker .

A police officer, stationed at the perimeter, approached to brief him. Saluting, he said, “Agent Williams, the protestors are demanding the release of Henry Parker . They claim he’s been wrongly imprisoned and are calling for a fair trial.”

Agent Williams, with an unreadable expression, surveyed the crowd. His keen eyes analyzed the intensity, the shouted slogans, and the emotions etched on every face. He nodded in acknowledgment to the officer.

The protest swelled like a turbulent sea, voices crashing against the walls of the government building. Positioned on the periphery, Agent Williams observed with vigilance. Amid the waves of dissent, he noticed a figure suspiciously fumbling with a bag and pulling out stones.

With determined strides, Agent Williams moved decisively into the crowd. His tall, imposing figure parted the mass, an embodiment of authority. As he approached the suspect, the imminent threat was swiftly neutralized.

With a deft move and a firm grip, Agent Williams intercepted the troublemaker. A yelp of pain momentarily rippled through the crowd, which momentarily silenced the chaotic uproar. Towering over the now-subdued troublemaker, Agent Williams spoke into a wireless mic, his voice cutting through the murmurs. "This is a call for peace," he declared, his authoritative tone resonating with the crowd. "Violence has no place here. We seek change through unity, not chaos."

A hush fell over the protesters, their energy subdued by his intervention. Standing center stage, Agent Williams reinforced his message: "Any act of violence will be met with consequences. Let this be a peaceful demonstration of our collective voice."

As law enforcement led the restrained troublemaker away, Agent Williams continued to monitor the crowd. His intervention had not only defused a potential crisis but also underscored the importance of peaceful protest. The protest continued under the vigilant eyes of the demonstrators and Agent Williams, now with a dynamic that favored change through harmony rather than discord.

In the afternoon, Agent Williams found himself in front of Victoria's apartment building, contemplating the gravity of the impending conversation. As his self-driving car hummed gently to a stop, he prepared himself to discuss the sensitive subjects that hung heavily between them.

Exiting the vehicle, Williams approached Victoria's apartment with a firm resolve. After a brief hesitation, he rang the doorbell. The chime echoed through the hallway, and as he waited, he steeled himself for the difficult encounter ahead.

The door opened to reveal Victoria, who greeted him with a warm but unsuspecting smile. Williams stepped into the dimly lit room, his tall silhouette imposing in the soft lighting, subtly altering the room's ambiance.

Victoria: "Williams, thank you for coming. It's been hectic with everything going on."

Williams: "Indeed, it's escalating daily. I know everyone is eager for Henry's release, but the protests might be counterproductive to his case."

Victoria, defensively: "But the protests are our voice. Henry is innocent, and we need the world to know."

Williams, calmly: "I understand, Victoria. And I want Henry free too. But we need to consider how this might affect his parole prospects. Demonstrations could portray a risk."

Victoria, frustrated: "So, what? We just do nothing?"

Williams: "Not at all. We need a strategic approach. Perhaps it's time to scale down the protests and focus on strengthening Henry's parole application."

Victoria, crossing her arms and walking towards the kitchen: "And let the system decide his fate while we stand by?"

Williams, gently: "We're not giving up, Victoria. We're focusing our efforts on what will most effectively secure his release. Let's gather strong character references and demonstrate his progress in rehabilitation programs."

Victoria, reluctantly feeding Ava in the high chair: "It feels like we're just waiting. Henry needs to know we're fighting."

Williams, compassionately: "He will. Our priority is to make a compelling case to the parole board that he's ready to reintegrate into society."

Their conversation continued, with Williams trying to reassure Victoria of the strategic shift. Meanwhile, Ava cooed softly, her attention on the pureed carrots Victoria fed her. The room was filled with the background hum of the TV until a breaking news alert caught Victoria's attention.

The news anchor announced a shocking assassination attempt on the Education Minister. As Victoria absorbed the gravity of the news, a sharp knock startled her. Turning toward the door, her expression shifted to fear as she saw uniformed officers standing outside.

In that moment, the serenity of feeding Ava was shattered by the harsh reality of the accusation that now loomed over Victoria. The spoon clattered to the floor as the officers approached, marking the beginning of a new, unforeseen crisis. In an instant, her life had been thrown into turmoil by a government known for silencing dissent.

As Victoria sat in the sterile interrogation room, her thoughts wandered to her daughter, Ava. She felt a pang of guilt, worrying about Ava's safety and well-being, despite knowing her brother, Agent Williams, was looking after her.

The door opened, and a government official she recognized from Henry's arrest entered. "Mrs. Parker ," he began formally, "we have reasons to suspect your involvement in your husband's activities, including a cryptic message on the dark web aimed at assassinating a minister."

Victoria's forehead beaded with sweat. "I don't know what you're talking about," she replied, her voice trembling slightly.

The official leaned in, his gaze intense. "We believe you are not just an accomplice but an active participant in the terrorist group your husband belonged to."

Feeling a sinking in her gut, Victoria whispered, "I'm innocent."

The man smirked. "That's what they all say. However, the evidence suggests otherwise. Prepare for a long stay in prison, Mrs. Parker ."

As the official left, despair washed over Victoria. She had known the risks of opposing the government, but the reality was far harsher than she had imagined.

That night, Agent Williams struggled to find peace in his sleep. The burdens of the day lingered, clouding his mind like a dense fog. In his dimly lit room, only the soft glow of a solitary lamp broke the darkness, casting long shadows that flickered against the walls. Beside him, Ava slept soundly, oblivious to the storm brewing in her guardian's subconscious.

As sleep finally embraced him, a surreal scene unfolded in his dreams. Darkness seemed to deepen, and a chilling presence emerged from the shadows. In his dream, a sinister, ebony snake slithered quietly towards him. Its scales shimmered with a menacing aura, reflecting a malevolent sheen that seemed almost otherworldly.

The serpent, a dark symbol of the threats they faced, coiled around Williams with a cold, eerie touch that sent shivers down his spine. The dream intensified, and he felt an overwhelming sense of danger as the snake moved towards Ava. Heart pounding with dread, he was helpless as the serpent struck, its fangs aiming for Ava.

Suddenly, Williams woke up, his body covered in a cold sweat. The room was now illuminated by the early morning light, a stark contrast to the ominous shadows of his nightmare. He gasped for air, his hands shaking as he reached out to ensure Ava was safe.

Relieved to find her unharmed, Williams sat back, the remnants of his nightmare lingering like echoes in his mind. His scars, earned from past battles, felt like they burned anew, each one a testament to the real and imagined wars he had fought.

The following morning, Williams found himself walking through the sterile, unwelcoming corridors of the prison to meet Victoria. The heavy metal doors clanged shut behind him, their echoes bouncing off the cold concrete walls. He entered the visiting area, where the harsh fluorescent lighting did little to warm the austere atmosphere.

Victoria settled into the hard, unforgiving chair, her fingers trembling slightly as she picked up the phone. Across the thick glass partition, Agent Williams lifted his receiver. Their eyes locked, a silent storm of shared pain and understanding swirling between them.

"Williams," Victoria's voice was a fragile whisper, quivering with the strain of emotions she fought to keep at bay. "I don't understand how it all came to this. Henry is locked away, and I'm entangled in accusations I know nothing about."

Agent Williams, whose face was usually an unreadable mask sculpted from years within the clandestine world, showed a flicker of raw emotion. The concern for her was palpable, etching lines of worry across his brow. "Victoria," he responded with a heavy sigh, "this was never the path I wanted for any of us. Henry, you, Ava... you shouldn't have to bear this burden."

As he spoke, Victoria's gaze inadvertently fell upon the myriad of scars crisscrossing his arms. Each was a silent testament to battles fought and sacrifices made. For a fleeting moment, their shared struggles transcended the physical barriers separating them, knitting them together in unspoken solidarity.

"Williams," Victoria continued, her voice breaking as desperation seeped through. "You have connections, resources. Can't you do something to help Henry and me? We don't belong behind these walls."

A momentary hesitation shadowed Williams' face. The scars he bore seemed to weigh him down, each a heavy reminder of duty and the cost it demanded. His eyes, deep and contemplative, met hers again, and she could see the inner conflict playing out behind them.

"Victoria, if it were only up to me," he began, his voice low and burdened with the weight of unseen obstacles, "I would tear down these walls. But the forces we're up against... they're not easily swayed, even by my own hands. But believe me, I will do everything within my power."

Victoria clutched the phone tighter, her knuckles white, as a tear escaped her control. "Please, Williams," she implored, each word soaked with urgency, "promise me you'll protect Ava. She's innocent in all this chaos. Get her out of Aurorium, away from the shadows of this government."

Above them, the lights flickered ominously, casting their faces in stark relief against the dreariness of the room. Williams exhaled deeply, a sound more felt than heard, resonating with the weight of promises in dangerous times. "I'm not sure how much I can manage from here, Victoria. They watch everything, even the shadows aren't safe. But for Henry, for you, and especially for Ava... I'll move heaven and earth."

Victoria's voice was barely a whisper now, edged with raw desperation. "Take her somewhere safe, somewhere they can't reach. Keep her safe, Williams. Please."

Williams nodded, the solemnity of his promise reflected in his gaze, heavy with the guilt of past decisions. "I'll do my best, Victoria. That's a promise. We can't rewrite our past, but I'll fight for Ava's future."

In the chilling stillness of the visiting room, their eyes met one last time, a silent vow passing through the glass that separated them. Each carried the weight of their choices, the burden of paths chosen and those forced upon them, a silent accord to strive against the tides that sought to sweep them away.

That night after meeting Victoria in the prison Agent Williams had meticulously crafted his plan to rescue Ava from the clutches of the oppressive Aurorium government. Under the veil of night, they embarked in his self-driving car, slipping through the city's shadowed arteries.

Ava, his niece, huddled in the back seat, her eyes wide with a blend of fear and anticipation. Outside, the city lights streaked past in a blur as they accelerated, with Williams keeping a vigilant eye on the omnipresent surveillance systems of Aurorium.

As they wove through the darkened city, an unsettling realization crept over Williams—the car was deviating from its intended course. What should have been a beacon of modern reliability, the car's autonomous system seemed to have succumbed to an external sabotage.

Panic clawed at Williams as he fought with the unresponsive controls. The steering wheel remained obstinate under his grip, refusing his desperate corrections. The car's speed, too, had escaped his command, betraying him at the most critical of moments.

Dread settled heavy in his chest. Had their escape been anticipated? Was this the work of unseen enemies? The grim truth dawned on him: their fight for freedom had been compromised, the very technology meant to aid their escape now a puppet to their adversaries.

In that harrowing moment of realization, the stakes became crystal clear. Their fate was being manipulated by shadowy forces intent on keeping them within Aurorium's grasp. The car, unchecked, hurtled toward an unknown destination—a terrifying uncertainty as their captor.

The night's silence was brutally shattered by the screech of metal as another self-driving car rammed into theirs. In the violent collision, the car's emergency protocols activated, deploying a protective capsule around Ava. It enveloped her in a secure embrace, shielding her from the chaos, a steadfast guardian against the treachery outside.

Williams, however, was not so fortunate. The impact left him battered and bruised, the severe injuries a testament to the perilous path of their escape. Amid the wreckage, his protective instincts for Ava remained undiminished, even as consciousness slipped away from him.

As the wail of emergency response drones filled the air, rushing to the scene, they found Williams unconscious, his form sprawled amidst the twisted metal. Ava, still encapsulated, cried softly, her tears a poignant echo of the night's terror.

Meanwhile, in the opulent office of the Education Minister, Mr. Smith savored a drink, the news of the night playing softly in the background. His solitude was interrupted by the insistent ring of his phone. It was Richard

Mercer, the Chief of Technology Security, with news of their operation's success.

"The job is done," Mercer reported succinctly.

A dark smile spread across Mr. Smith 's face as he absorbed the confirmation of their plot's fruition. "Excellent work, Richard," he responded, a cold satisfaction in his voice. Their covert machinations had borne the intended outcome, sealing the fates of those who dared to defy them.

5

The Unforgivable Law

After 20 years, on a chilly night in Nebula Vista city, the clock struck 9:45 PM, casting long shadows across the deserted streets. A sleek police car stopped in front of a suburban home, from which emerged a humanoid RoboCop, a marvel of modern technology. Its eyes, devoid of emotion, scanned the building, detecting the warmth of human life inside—right down to a woman, expectant with a child.

"All clear," the RoboCop announced.

Following its signal, human officers, masked and armed, approached the house. They were greeted at the door by a middle-aged man, Jake, whose face was etched with confusion.

"Officers, how can I help you?" Jake inquired, his voice steady but his hands betraying a slight tremor.

"Hello Jake, I'm Agent Williams," replied the lead officer, a smile flickering across his lips as he stepped inside. The other officers followed, their boots thumping softly against the wooden floor.

"Lovely house," Williams commented, his tone casual but his eyes sharp and assessing. "We're just here for a routine check. I hope you don't mind."

Jake nodded, though his anxiety was palpable. "Of course. Honey, could you come here?" he called out.

His wife, Natasha, entered the room, her expression one of wary curiosity. "Yes, I'm Natasha. What's this about?"

"We're conducting a routine check. There's been a slight issue with suspects evading our surveillance," Williams explained, his voice calm.

Natasha clung to Jake, her voice trembling. "Should we be worried?"

"Please, there's no need for alarm. The suspects aren't dangerous. But I do have a few questions," Williams reassured them, though his gaze was intrusive, more so than the situation warranted.

The conversation shifted unexpectedly as Williams mentioned their unborn child. "I see you're expecting—congratulations. Boy or girl?"

"It's a boy," Jake replied, his pride momentarily overshadowing his nervousness.

Williams's next request, however, sent a chill through the room. "I'd love to see him now. We have the technology to do that," he said, stepping closer to Natasha.

Natasha backed away, her fear evident. "I'm not comfortable with this. I want you to leave."

Williams's tone hardened. "That's not how you treat guests." "We didn't invite you," Natasha retorted, her voice firm despite her fear.

Ignoring her protest, Williams signaled his team to proceed. A scanner was deployed, but the situation quickly escalated. Jake tried to intervene, only to be restrained by the officers. The scanner whirred to life, revealing not only the baby's details but also the true identities of the couple, hidden under disguises.

"Looks like it's a girl," Williams said, a smirk playing on his lips. "And you are not who you claim to be."

The couple's fear turned to despair as their true identities—Jude and Thomas—were exposed.

The cold, metallic cuffs clamped around Thomas's wrists with an ominous finality. He was led down the stark, echoing hallway by guards whose faces were set in stern, unyielding lines. As he walked, Thomas's voice broke the oppressive silence, his plea desperate and raw. "Please, don't harm my wife and the baby. Let them go."

Simultaneously, in a dimly lit corridor of a distant hospital, Jude was confined to a stretcher, her wrists and ankles strapped down with chilling efficiency. The sterile walls magnified the ominous squeak of the stretcher's wheels as it glided toward the operation theatre. The hospital staff, faces obscured behind surgical masks, marched alongside, indifferent to the emotional tumult they escorted. Jude's cries—filled with a mother's terror at the potential loss of her unborn child—echoed down the hallway, "No, please don't kill my baby." Her pleas were muffled as the heavy doors of the theatre swung shut, but her despair lingered, a haunting refrain in the empty corridor.

Meanwhile, Agent Williams entered the stark prison corridor with a calculated air of authority. His boots clinked against the cold, hard floor, a sound as cold as his heart. He stopped at Thomas's cell, observing the man whose life he had irrevocably altered. Thomas sat on the edge of his cot, his face buried in his hands, his shoulders shaking from silent sobs.

With a flick of his lighter, Williams ignited a cigarette, the smoke curling upwards in the stale air. He offered the pack to Thomas with a nonchalant gesture. "Care for one?" His voice was as cold as the walls surrounding them. Thomas, caught in the throes of his anguish, barely looked up, his spirit shattered.

"As for your situation," Williams began, the smoke veiling his face, "you cannot appeal this. You're looking at five years, and it will decimate your social score. Starting over won't be easy." His tone was matter-of-fact, as if discussing something as mundane as the weather.

"Planning a child is not a crime," Thomas countered, his voice hoarse with grief and anger.

"That's where you're wrong," Williams replied coolly. "You need to align with the government's policies to survive. Anyone who opposes will face consequences."

Thomas's eyes, red and swollen, met Williams's with a look of helpless fury. His dreams, once filled with the joy of impending fatherhood, now lay in ruins.

Williams turned to leave, but not before delivering one final blow. "By the way, the surgery is done. Your wife is stable. You won't have to worry about this kind of trouble again," he said, his words laced with a chilling finality that suggested an irreversible change.

As Williams's footsteps receded, Thomas slid to the floor, the cold of the iron bars seeping into his bones. The revelation of his wife's surgery and the irreversible alteration of their future weighed heavily upon him, a burden too profound to bear. His cries, muffled by the walls of his cell, were a heart-wrenching testament to the cruelty of their fate.

6

The Debate

In the cozy warmth of their small apartment, bathed in the soft glow of morning light, Chloe moved gracefully around the kitchen, crafting a delightful breakfast. The rich aroma of freshly brewed coffee mingled with the comforting sizzle of eggs.

Jann, dressed in simple work clothes, flicked on the TV with practiced ease. As the screen came alive, the buzz of the morning news filled the room, drawing Chloe's attention even amidst her culinary dance.

The news cut to a heated debate on the government's controversial child planning law, a topic that hung in the air like a looming storm. Chloe's movements slowed, each clink of the cutlery against the plates laden with a sense of foreboding as she considered the law's impact on their dreams of parenthood.

The newsroom hummed with the electric tension of a live debate, its stage set for a pivotal discourse on the contentious new child planning law. The host introduced the first speaker, Politician 1, whose voice rang with vehemence as he denounced the law.

Politician 1: "This new law egregiously strips the populace of their basic right to decide when to have children. It is not the place of any government to make such intimate decisions for its citizens."

Across the stage, Politician 2 stood ready, his stance firm as he prepared to offer a contrasting viewpoint.

Politician 2: "Your perspective overlooks a critical issue—our dwindling natural resources. Without measures to control population growth, we risk widespread starvation and possible extinction. This law is a necessary step to avoid a dire future. Moreover, it aims to reduce inflation and societal issues by encouraging a population that can contribute positively to society."

Politician 1 scoffed in disbelief. "Are you implying that criminal tendencies are linked to lower intelligence?"

Politician 2: "That's an oversimplification. While not all individuals with lower IQs engage in criminal activity, statistical data suggest a correlation. This law seeks to mitigate such risks by fostering environments that promote education and proper upbringing, thereby reducing crime."

Politician 1 countered sharply, "Recent statistics from states where this law has been long implemented show a predominance of births in the privileged classes, with scant representation from the underprivileged. This clearly indicates a bias that favors the affluent."

Politician 2 retorted, "That interpretation is flawed. The statistics actually demonstrate effective control of population quality, which ensures that future generations can positively impact society."

The debate quickly escalated as they delved into the disparities between social classes.

Politician 1 pressed on, "If this is truly about equality, why do we see such a stark disparity in educational opportunities between privileged and underprivileged children?"

Politician 2, undeterred, replied, "It's a matter of economic capability. Parents must have the means to afford prestigious schools if they wish for a better future for their children."

Politician 1 then highlighted the broader economic repercussions, "This law perpetuates a cycle where the underprivileged remain stuck in low wage jobs, barred from advancing. Meanwhile, the cost of living soars, further discouraging them from having children. This isn't just biased; it's a tool for maintaining a class-based hierarchy."

Politician 2 maintained a staunch defense of the government's role, "The government is actively supporting the underprivileged with allowances and subsidies. It's easy to criticize, but constructive contributions are scarce. This debate is devolving into fruitlessness."

With those final words, Politician 2 abruptly ended his participation, taking the microphone with him as he exited. He left behind a charged atmosphere, resonating with the clash of deeply divided opinions that continued to echo through the newsroom.

Back at the apartment, the debate struck a chord with Chloe. As she set the table, her voice trembled slightly, "Jann, maybe it's time we think about having a child. What's your take?"

Jann, his expression grave as he absorbed the weight of the debate, replied, "With our financial struggles, can we really afford to bring a child into this world?"

Tears brimmed in Chloe's eyes as the weight of their situation sank in. "But I earn too, and surely, we can make it work," she insisted, more to reassure herself.

Jann took her hands in his, his voice gentle yet tinged with realism, "It's not just about money, Chloe. It's about providing a life where our child can thrive."

Resolved to face their challenges together, Jann promised, "Let's apply for approval today. I'll handle it."

As the amber hues of the evening sky spilled through the window, Chloe sat by the small table, her fingers anxiously twisting the hem of her shirt. The silence of their modest home felt heavier than usual, broken only by the occasional creak of the floorboards. She kept glancing at the door, her heart thudding with a mix of anticipation and dread.

When Jann finally walked in, his shoulders slumped and his eyes fixed on the ground, she knew the answer before he even spoke. He lingered by the doorway, his hand still resting on the handle, as if the weight of what he carried was too much to bear.

"Our application…" he began, his voice barely above a whisper. He took a deep breath, then forced the words out. "It was denied. They said there's no suitable position in the future that matches… our baby's potential skills."

The room seemed to shrink around them, the air thick with the crushing blow of his statement. Chloe's breath hitched, but her spirit—unyielding even in despair—refused to falter. She stood, her eyes blazing with determination.

"Then we'll appeal," she declared, her voice cutting through the gloom like a blade. "We can't just let them decide our future for us. We won't."

Jann stepped forward, the frustration in his expression softened by the admiration he felt for her resilience. He ran a hand through his hair, exhaling deeply, as if searching for words strong enough to match hers.

"Chloe," he said, his voice steady but laced with an undercurrent of desperation. "We'll find a way. I promise you. Together."

She reached out, her hand brushing his arm, but before she could respond, he continued, his tone shifting to something almost conspiratorial.

"There is… another way," he began hesitantly. His eyes flickered with uncertainty. "A network. They operate in secret. They can help us… have a child. But—" He paused, the weight of what he was about to say visible in his furrowed brow. "We'd have to relocate. To Aurorium City."

Chloe's lips parted, but no words came immediately. The mention of Aurorium City—the sprawling, glittering metropolis shrouded in whispers of danger and opportunity—sent a chill down her spine.

"How would we even survive there?" she finally asked, her voice tinged with worry. "We don't have jobs. Our savings wouldn't last long, Jann. What if—"

"They'll take care of it," he cut her off, though his voice carried no assurance, only hope. "That's what they promised. They'll cover everything."

Chloe crossed her arms, her brows knitting as doubt crept into her thoughts. "And you trust them? A secret network willing to upend our lives? What if it's all… too good to be true?"

Jann looked away for a moment, as if grappling with his own doubts. "I don't know," he admitted, his voice dropping to a whisper. "But… this is the best shot we've got. If we want this—if we want a family—we have to take the chance."

For a moment, the room was silent but for the distant hum of the city outside their window. Chloe studied him, her heart torn between fear of the unknown and the desperate hope that he might be right.

Finally, she stepped forward and pulled him into a tight embrace, her face buried in his shoulder. "Then we'll face it together," she murmured, her voice steady despite the storm brewing inside her. "Whatever it takes."

Jann wrapped his arms around her, holding on as if she was his anchor. No more words were exchanged, but the unspoken vow between them was clear: they would face the uncertainty ahead with unity and love, no matter where it led them.

7

The Murder

In Aurorium City, the towering monoliths of the government's skyscrapers reached defiantly toward the heavens, their imposing forms casting ominous shadows over the bustling metropolis. These colossal structures, like metallic giants, stood as a symbol of authority and control.

As the radiant bright day attempted to bathe the city in its celestial glow, the colossal silhouettes of these skyscrapers intercepted its light, creating an intricate dance of shadows that sprawled across the urban landscape. The city found itself ensconced in a perpetual twilight, the stark contrast between the bright daylight and shadowed areas reflecting the stark divide in power and influence.

The shadows of these immense buildings extended far and wide, engulfing streets, parks, and residential areas, creating a stark visual metaphor for the overarching control the government exerted. The citizens of Aurorium moved about their daily lives, shrouded in the penumbra cast by these monolithic structures, a constant reminder of the authoritative presence that loomed above them. The ethereal dance between light and shadow became an integral part of the city's aesthetic, an unintended consequence of the government's insatiable appetite for dominance.

In a futuristic dystopian world, where the government has complete control over every aspect of citizens' lives, skyscrapers tower over the city, and advanced technologies like police drones and holographic displays are commonplace. But behind the gleaming facade, there is a sense of oppression and unease that hangs over the city like a cloud. Life is a constant struggle between those who seek freedom and those who seek control. Citizens must navigate a complex web of laws and regulations.

On a brisk Monday morning in Aurorium, the town hall brimmed with anticipation as media representatives gathered for a crucial press conference. The imposing figure of Mayor Johnson , known for his commanding presence, approached the podium with a measured stride. Clearing his throat, he surveyed the room with a steely gaze.

"Good morning, citizens of Aurorium," his voice boomed, echoing off the walls. "Today, we discuss a pivotal new law regarding family planning, crafted to guide our community toward a sustainable future."

A ripple of murmurs swept through the crowd, reporters leaning in as the air thickened with intrigue.

"This law mandates governmental approval for all couples desiring to bear children," the mayor announced, igniting a collective gasp from the assembly. A flurry of questions erupted, slicing through the charged atmosphere.

"Please, let me explain before we proceed with questions," Mayor Johnson continued, raising a hand to quell the rising tide of voices. "This legislation does not curtail freedom but ensures our growth is manageable and mindful, aligning with our broader goals of enhanced healthcare, educational excellence, and societal prosperity."

The room fell into a contentious silence as he detailed the envisioned benefits: healthier children, reduced crime, and a flourishing society.

"We recognize the contentious nature of this law," he admitted, locking eyes with his audience, "but its success in other regions has shown promising outcomes. We are dedicated to facilitating this transition with transparency and support."

A journalist stood, tension palpable in his voice. "Isn't this an infringement on our personal freedom?"

A slight smile touched the mayor's lips as he responded, "On the contrary, it's a protective measure. By managing birth rates, we ensure every child access to necessary resources, laying the groundwork for a fair and just society."

The questions continued, probing the implications of the law.

"How will you enforce this without infringing on personal liberties?" another reporter challenged.

"Our strategy hinges on education and voluntary compliance, supported by safe birth control methods. Enforcement will be a last resort, reserved for those who blatantly disregard the regulations," the mayor explained, his tone firm yet reassuring.

"And what of discrimination? How will you prevent it from affecting the disadvantaged or those with disabilities?" the next question came, sharp and quick.

"Every measure has been taken to guarantee fair and equitable treatment for all citizens, ensuring everyone has equal access to family planning services," he asserted, the conviction in his voice unwavering.

"On what parameters Government would approve to have a child?" another reporter questioned.

Mayor: Government believes that certain skills and abilities would be more in demand in the future than others, and that it was important to ensure that the population was able to meet these demands. Therefore, the government would use genetic testing to determine the potential skills and abilities of the child based on their parents' genes, and then determine whether these skills would be required in the future based on predictions of the job market and technological advancements.

If the child was deemed to have the potential to possess skills that would be in high demand in the future, the government would be more likely to approve the couple's request to have a child. On the other hand, if the child was not predicted to possess the desired skillset, applicant's request will be rejected.

One of the most important parameters is income. People who can afford to have children without relying on government assistance are more likely to be approved for family planning. Couples who were below a certain income threshold or hold financial liabilities were likely to be denied approval, as the government did not want to risk burdening the welfare system with additional dependents.

Another parameter is health. Couples who have medical conditions that could potentially put the mother or the child at risk during pregnancy or childbirth will be denied approval. This is to protect the health of the mother and the child and to prevent additional strain on the healthcare system.

Age is also a factor that the government would consider. Couples who were deemed too young or too old to have children would often be denied approval. This was done to prevent risks associated with young mothers or complications that could arise with older mothers.

Finally, the government also considered the number of children a couple already had. Couples who had more than the allowed number of children were often denied approval for family planning. This was done to prevent overpopulation and to ensure that resources were being used effectively.

The conference neared its end under a cloud of relentless inquiry.

"Thank you for your questions. Further details will be provided in due course," Mayor Johnson concluded, signaling the close of the session. The reporters' pens raced across notepads, capturing the last of his words as the murmurs resumed, a storm of debate brewing over Aurorium.

In the shadows of a nearby parking garage, a mysterious woman watched, her eyes sharp and calculating. As the mayor moved toward his vehicle amid a swirl of security and clamoring journalists, she sensed her moment drawing near. With a quiet determination, she readied herself, aware that the time to act was fast approaching.

Under the cloak of an ordinary day, the mysterious woman had orchestrated her most daring act. She wielded a remote, activating a robotic insect so artfully crafted it could have fooled any onlooker. Disguised as a benign fly, this tiny automaton was engineered with cutting edge technology, including a minuscule syringe primed with a lethal, untraceable neurotoxin.

With a subtle flick of her wrist, she dispatched the robotic assailant into the bustling air. It mingled flawlessly with the swarm of real insects, its silent wings carrying it deftly toward its unsuspecting target—the Mayor.

Amidst the fervor of his departure, as the Mayor waved to the gathered crowd and moved toward his vehicle, the insect struck. It expertly navigated the chaos and injected the poison into his left ankle with a precision that belied its mechanical nature. The toxin, deliberately chosen for its slow-acting properties, would mimic the gradual toll of natural ailments, deflecting any immediate suspicion.

Inside his car, the Mayor remained oblivious to the sinister orchestration, feeling no more than a tickle at his ankle. Meanwhile, the woman, her heart pounding with a cocktail of adrenaline and relief, discreetly vanished into the throng. Her face was just another blur in the crowd, her sinister role unnoticed.

As the toxin began its deadly work, it would slowly unravel the Mayor's health, manifesting symptoms that seemed innocuous and unrelated. The woman had calculated every detail, ensuring the poison's effects would peak when no eyes would suspect her involvement.

With the deed now behind her, the woman slipped away into the shadowy arteries of the city, leaving no trace but the impending chaos of her actions. She moved through the streets, a spectre of revolution, knowing well that the reverberations of this day would ignite the transformative fire she sought. The city, unbeknownst to its dwellers, stood on the precipice of upheaval.

8

The Serpent

News of Mayor Johnson's untimely death cascaded through the city of Aurorium, igniting a maelstrom of confusion and chaos within the government and among the populace. The city, usually a beacon of futuristic calm with its silent, magnetically-guided vehicles and bustling drones, was now a hotbed of anxiety and speculation. Citizens were left pondering the ramifications of this sudden vacuum of power and the inevitable shifts that might follow.

On the crowded sidewalks, under the watchful eyes of hovering drones, the city's heartbeat seemed to quicken. Each person, regardless of their walk of life, seemed to carry a mix of dread and expectation.

News Anchor: "We're live on the streets of Aurorium, capturing the public's reaction to Mayor Johnson's shocking demise. Let's hear what the citizens have to say."

The news team navigated through the throng, their cameras picking up the raw emotions of the crowd.

Citizen 1, tears welling up: "It's a profound loss. Mayor Johnson championed our causes. We demand justice for this vile act!"

Citizen 2, with a tone of bitterness: "It's a reflection of our deteriorating city. It's time the authorities own up to the mess they've allowed to fester."

The anchors continued, their questions painting a vivid portrait of a city divided in grief and discontent.

News Anchor, turning to another bystander: "Sir, how do you see the future unfolding from here?"

Citizen 3, looking visibly troubled: "I'm concerned for our city's stability. We can't afford more upheaval."

News Anchor, addressing another passerby: "Ma'am, any thoughts on the impact of these recent events?"

Citizen 4, frustrated: "The government's policies have brought us to this point. Maybe now, they'll finally listen."

News Anchor, concluding: "As the investigation into Mayor Johnson's death progresses, Aurorium finds itself at a crucial juncture. The citizens, each echoing unique sentiments, are clamouring for answers and decisive action from their leaders. This is a city at the brink, its glossy facade barely containing the simmering unrest beneath. Back to you in the studio."

In the wake of the tragedy, the general public, caught in this urban tempest, shared their fears and frustrations, painting a poignant picture of a city on edge. The government, scrambling to restore order, ramped up security measures, casting a vigilant eye over the cityscape to pre-empt any further disruptions.

Mayor Johnson's death reverberated through the foundations of Aurorium's society and governance, fueling a climate ripe with uncertainty and calls for change. As the city teetered, the future hung in balance, with the government struggling to steady a ship rocked by sudden loss and rising public dissent.

The hum of tension filled the air as the city's most influential figures filed into the futuristic meeting room deep within the heart of Aurorium's government complex. As everyone entered, the smart glass walls—clear as a crystal lake—shifted from transparency to a frosted, impenetrable barrier at the wave of the first official's hand. The shift was immediate, a subtle reminder that what was about to be discussed was meant for no ears beyond these walls.

The large, oval table at the center was made of a single piece of reflective black material that seemed to absorb light. It was surrounded by ergonomic chairs. The politicians, a diverse group representing the city's multifaceted demographics, were dressed in attire that balanced traditional formal wear.

The austere government chamber echoed with hushed conversations as high-ranking officials and politicians gathered to address the pressing matters before them. The air was thick with tension and uncertainty, each individual contemplating the gravity of the situation. The expressions around the table were a mix of determination and anxiety. Wrinkles of worry were etched on foreheads, and eyes darted with restless energy. Every so often, a politician would adjust their attire, a nervous gesture betraying their inner turmoil.

Politician 1: (leaning forward) "The death of the Mayor has left a void, and the public is demanding answers. We need to discuss the investigation and the impending elections for a new mayor."

Politician 2: (firmly) "Security protocols need to be revisited. We can't afford another incident. We must ensure the safety of our officials."

Politician 3: "The public is in turmoil. We need to handle this delicately. A new mayor must bring stability."

Richard Mercer: (addressing the room) "We need a candidate for the upcoming elections. This city can't function without leadership."

A palpable sense of reluctance filled the room. No one seemed eager to step into the shoes of the late mayor, knowing the risks associated with such a position. The death of the Mayor created a power vacuum within the government. The remaining officials scrambled to fill the void and maintain the functioning of the city's administration.

Richard Mercer, the Director of the Aurorium Security Bureau, made his way through the dimly lit, hushed corridors of the police command center, his polished shoes echoing softly on the sleek, dark floor. He was headed towards one particular office with name board "Agent Williams", one that was somewhat secluded from the others.

Agent Williams' office was a blend of minimalist design and high-tech functionality. The walls were a soothing shade of grey, lined with digital screens displaying various data feeds and security footage from across the city. One entire wall was a transparent smart glass looking out onto a serene garden, a contrast to the high-stakes work that filled the room. The furniture was sparse but elegant, with a large, sturdy desk made of recycled composite materials dominating the space.

Sitting behind the desk was Agent Williams, a figure of calm and focus. His expression was one of intense concentration as he reviewed files on his holographic display, but he looked up as he sensed Mercer's presence, his eyes sharp and alert.

"Richard." Williams greeted, his voice even and welcoming, though his posture remained alert, a subtle indication of the respect he held for the chain of command and the seriousness of any visit by the Director.

Mercer closed the door gently behind him and took a seat across from Williams. His face was drawn, the lines around his eyes more pronounced than usual—a clear sign of the burdens he carried. "Williams, I wouldn't be here if it weren't urgent. We've got a situation that requires your particular set of skills."

Williams nodded, his face set into a mask of professionalism, yet a flicker of curiosity passed through his eyes. "I'm listening, sir."

"It's about the Mayor— He's dead." Mercer stated bluntly, observing Williams closely for a reaction.

A slight tension flickered across Williams' face, but his training kept any shock from lingering. "Understood. How did it happen?"

"We're not sure yet, and that's the problem. It's being treated as a homicide. Given your expertise in such investigations and your ability to stay under the radar, you're the best we have for this delicate matter," Mercer explained, his voice low and serious.

Williams leaned back, his mind already racing through the possibilities, his expression one of focused determination. "What's the priority here, Richard? Truth or stability?"

Mercer sighed, the weight of the decision evident in his pause. "Both, if possible. But truth first. We need to know if this was political, personal, or something else. This city is a tinderbox, Williams, and this incident might just be the spark. We need answers fast, and we need them to be right."

Williams nodded, a firm set to his jaw. "You'll have your answers. I'll need access to all the resources we've got—surveillance, forensics, intel, everything."

"You'll have it." Mercer assured him. His gaze held Williams', a silent exchange of trust and acknowledgment of the stakes involved.

As Mercer stood to leave, he placed a reassuring hand on Williams' shoulder, a rare personal gesture that spoke volumes of his respect and trust in Williams' abilities. "Keep me updated, Williams. And be careful."

"I always am." Williams replied, a slight, wry smile touching his lips as he turned back to his screens, already mentally plotting his first moves in the investigation.

As the door clicked shut, the office returned to its quiet state, with Agent Williams now fully absorbed in the gravity and challenge of the task ahead. His face was a mask of resolve, the gears of his analytical mind turning rapidly, ready to unravel the mystery of the Mayor's death.

In the murky corridors of power, where shadows cast long and whispers travel far, Agent Williams was known as the silent orchestrator. As protests escalated and the government's confusion intensified like a gathering storm, Williams expanded his control, turning chaos into his canvas.

The day of reckoning arrived under a cloud of uncertainty. High-ranking officials, their expressions a complex tapestry of frustration and curiosity, convened urgently. Agent Williams entered the meeting room belatedly, his stride exuding a mastery of the unfolding drama. He took his seat with an air of dismissive nonchalance, ignoring the customary greetings. His arrogance simmered in the room, sparking a palpable resentment among the assembled officials.

One bold official, unable to contain his irritation, demanded, "Agent Williams, your tardiness requires an explanation. What kept you?"

Leaning back with a mischievous glint in his eyes, Williams replied, "My apologies for the delay, but I've been unravelling a rather riveting piece of our city's hidden narrative."

He proceeded to captivate the room with his revelations. "This morning, I delved deeper into the city's underbelly and discovered unsettling connections involving a high-ranking official." he paused, letting the implication hang heavily in the air. He described how he had uncovered compromising material that not only threatened to scandalize but also implicated the official in a clandestine child trafficking network.

"As I explored these dark corners, I unearthed evidence that could detonate not only the career but also the personal life of one of our colleagues here." Williams continued, his voice steady, each word dropping like a stone in the stillness of the room. He skillfully kept the official's identity shrouded, magnifying the suspense.

The initial indignation over his late arrival and perceived disrespect dissolved into a stunned silence. Minds raced, and eyes darted, as officials silently speculated about the identity of the implicated colleague.

"Now, the question isn't about my tardiness; it's about the severe misjudgments and entanglements that have come to light. We must address these with the gravity they demand." Williams concluded, his tone firm, leaving the room tethered to his narrative.

He rose, his presence commanding as he walked around to face them all. A confident smirk played on his lips, signaling the completion of his power play. "It's not merely about quelling protests. It's about mastering their tempo. As the conductor of this intricate symphony, I assure you, interference would only result in dissonance."

With those final words, Agent Williams exited, leaving a room fraught with tension and uncertainty. The officials, now painfully aware of the precariousness of their positions, were left to ponder the profound implications of challenging the master tactician who now held sway over the city's fate. The silent message was clear: in the intricate game of power, Williams was not just a player but the composer, and the symphony was far from over.

9

The Protests

In the city's cacophony of protests, Agent Williams moved like a spectre, his presence barely noticed yet deeply felt. He identified the linchpins of each demonstration, those whose influence could sway public opinion. Among them was Elena Rodriguez, a charismatic activist studying astrophysics, whose family's clinic serving the underprivileged provided a potential pressure point. Then there was Malik Khan, a tech manager whose family's health crises he catalogued as leverage. Olivia Chang's participation in a mental health support group, Carlos Gomez's brother's undocumented status, and Kevin Miller's financially precarious restaurant venture were all threads in the vast web Williams wove.

These individuals, diverse in their passions yet united in their cause, unknowingly had their vulnerabilities catalogued by Williams. Each piece of information was a weapon in his arsenal, held back only until the moment to strike was ripe. In the background, Williams played a strategic game, each move calculated to bring him closer to domination.

The surveillance operations room, situated in the bowels of a nondescript government building, was a place of shadows and whispers, where the city's secrets were laid bare under the watchful eyes of Agent Williams and his team. The room was bathed in the blue glow of multiple large screens, each displaying streams of data, live video feeds, and complex networks of personal connections. In the center of the room, a holographic display projected a 3D model of the city, with various points of interest highlighted in pulsing red.

Agent Williams stood before the holographic cityscape, his silhouette sharp against the digital glow. Around him, his team members were stationed at their respective terminals, their faces set in expressions of intense concentration. The air was thick with the gravity of their task—monitoring Elena Rodriguez, an activist whose influence was growing dangerously potent.

"Report," Williams commanded, his voice cutting through the low hum of computers and soft clicking of keyboards.

A young analyst, her eyes reflecting the stark light of the display she monitored, stood to deliver her findings. "Sir, Elena's routine has been consistent. She's punctual at her university classes in the morning, spends early afternoons either at the library or in meetings with fellow activists. Evenings are dedicated to her community work. Her movements are predictable to a degree, but she maintains a cautious profile, often changing meeting venues at the last moment."

A team member spoke urgently. "We've analyzed her social media. Her posts align with upcoming protests and drive significant engagement. She's influential but careful, never revealing too much."

On the main screen, a map zoomed into the university campus, showing Elena walking briskly, her face resolute. Adjacent screens displayed intercepted texts and calls, dissecting her digital footprint.

Williams, eyes on the screens, asked, "Her vulnerabilities?"

The psychological profiler adjusted his glasses. "Her brother's clinic. It's her emotional anchor and Achilles' heel. Threats there could destabilize her, make her predictable."

Silence filled the room as the gravity of their mission sank in. Williams circled the holographic display, studying her frequented spots. Finally, he ordered, "Initiate phase two. Start subtle disruptions at the clinic. Monitor her response. I want to see how she handles pressure."

The team, resolute yet solemn, turned back to their tasks as the operations room buzzed with calculated intensity, poised to test the resilience of a rising activist.

In the bustling heart of downtown, a sea of determined protestors raised their voices in unified dissent, their placards painting a vivid scene of defiance against the urban backdrop. Amid the largest rally yet, Elena Rodriguez stood at its core, her voice resonating through amplifiers, igniting waves of cheers. Charismatic and commanding, she had become the unspoken leader, inspiring thousands under the grey sky with her call for change.

The placards were as diverse as the crowd itself, each one a bold statement against the contentious Child Planning Law. "Freedom to Choose," one declared in bold, defiant letters. Another read, "Our Children, Our Decision," waving like a banner of rebellion in the slight breeze. Yet another placard, vibrant with hand-painted colors, demanded, "End Government Overreach!"

Protestors from all walks of life gathered, their voices rising in unison against legislation they believed threatened their futures and family autonomy. "Rights, not regulations!" and "Hands off our families!" echoed through the streets, their chants filling the air with urgency and resolve. Strangers united in solidarity, their shared purpose forging instant connections, even as the city's daily life pulsed around them.

Above, digital billboards flickered, but the true message was in their defiance. This wasn't just a protest—it was a fight for principles and personal freedom, a stand they were prepared to sustain.

Meanwhile, miles away, Agent Williams watched the rally from a secure vehicle, his face unreadable. At his command, a calculated move was executed: Elena's brother, a dedicated gynecologist, was arrested on fabricated charges. The blow was precise, striking Elena at her core—her family.

As Elena raised her hand to signal the crowd's silence for a moment of respect for those who had suffered under the current regime, her phone vibrated insistently in her pocket. With a frown, she excused herself from the podium, weaving through the sea of bodies to a quieter spot under the skeletal branches of a leafless tree.

Her father's voice was choked with emotion as he relayed the news. "Elena, it's your brother," he stammered, the words heavy and uncertain. "He's been arrested. They're saying—it's serious, Elena."

The phone almost slipped from her trembling hands. Her brother, the gentlest soul she knew, accused of such a vile act? It couldn't be. But the timing, the precision of the strike—it reeked of manipulation. Her mind raced, connecting dots with a painful clarity.

Elena's face, usually a beacon of resolve and strength, crumpled under the weight of personal anguish and betrayal. She leaned against the tree, her body momentarily weak. Around her, the rally continued, but its leader was momentarily lost, swallowed by a storm of personal crisis.

With Elena distracted and her focus shattered, the cohesion of the rally began to fray. Confusion spread through the crowd as whispers of their leader's sudden departure turned into rumors. The unity began to unravel, the collective energy dissipating like smoke.

As the rally for the Child Planning law gained momentum, a giant billboard flickered to life, displaying a shocking headline: "Local Doctor Arrested for Misconduct." The image of Elena's brother, confused and fearful, filled the screen. The news stunned the crowd, turning their energy from support for the law to outrage.

"Can you believe this? In our community!" one protester exclaimed. "It's a setup," another argued. "Why now, during the rally?"

Anger spread, and some protesters began marching toward the community clinic, once a symbol of hope, now targeted by suspicions. Chanting "No more secrets! No more lies!" they gathered outside, demanding answers and justice.

Elena, meanwhile, was torn between the rally and her brother's plight. Hearing of the growing protest at the clinic, she felt her resolve harden. Racing to the site, she found herself confronted not only by the police and media but by faces she recognized—people who had stood by her at countless other rallies, now looking at her with suspicion and anger.

"Elena! How can you lead us when your own house is in disorder?" a former ally called out, the disappointment in his voice striking Elena harder than any accusation.

Facing the crowd, Elena raised her hands, a plea for calm and understanding. "Please, let's not jump to conclusions. We know nothing yet," she implored, her voice steady despite the turmoil within.

The damage was done. Seeds of doubt were sown, fracturing the rally's unity and diverting its energy. As Elena struggled to mend the gap, Agent Williams watched from afar, grimly satisfied. The protest wasn't just disrupted; it was manipulated, turning protesters against one another. The billboard, a cold harbinger of doubt, proved the power of perception over truth.

Williams' next target was Kevin Miller, a passionate advocate for justice, yet vulnerable to Williams' ruthless tactics. As darkness enveloped the city, Williams left the rally, already plotting Kevin's downfall.

In Kevin's bustling restaurant, where savory spices filled the air, a solitary figure sat in the shadows, his sharp gaze out of place amid the cheerful crowd. Spotting the stranger, Kevin's practiced smile faltered as he approached, blending warmth with caution. "Good evening, sir. Is everything to your satisfaction?"

The man, whose features were sharp and calculating, simply nodded before gesturing to the seat opposite him. "Sit, Kevin," his voice was low, laced with an unyielding edge that was impossible to ignore. Confusion knitted Kevin's brow, but he complied, sliding into the booth.

Leaning forward, the man's eyes pierced into Kevin's, an unspoken threat weaving through their locked gazes. "Your restaurant is flourishing, Kevin," he began, his voice a controlled murmur that seemed to carve out a private sphere amidst the public setting. "But such success doesn't go unnoticed."

Kevin's discomfort grew, a knot tightening in his stomach. He nodded silently, urging the man to continue.

"I've taken a particular interest in your finances," the man continued, his tone even but underlaid with a cold precision. "Your tax records, Kevin, they tell a compelling story—one of discrepancies."

A bead of sweat slid down Kevin's temple. "I—I've paid all my taxes. Everything's in order," he stammered.

The man chuckled darkly. "Perception often outweighs truth. And yours isn't favorable. Your protests against the government—noble, but dangerous."

Kevin's eyes widened. "How do you know about that?" he whispered.

The man's unsettling smile deepened. "Elena Rodriguez thought she was doing the right thing too, until it all fell apart. Focus on your restaurant, Kevin. Leave the protests, or you'll lose more than you can imagine."

With that, the man left, the door's bell jingling softly as Kevin sat frozen, anxiety clawing at his thoughts.

In a dim operations room, Agent Williams monitored a digital map displaying city protests against the child planning law. Fiery red dots scattered the screen, signaling unrest.

Over days, the red dots dimmed—first orange, then blue—marking a decline in protests. Williams, calm and calculating, directed his team to exploit vulnerabilities and quash dissent.

Within a week, the red dots representing protests on the city map began to fade. Slowly, the demonstrations came to an end. People returned to their daily lives, their enthusiasm and hopes seemed lost.

Elena tried her best to prove her brother's innocence, but the legal process was long and exhausting. Distrust and fear among her supporters shook the foundation of her movement. She began to feel like a leader abandoned by her own people.

On the other hand, Kevin Miller made a hard decision in his silence. To save his restaurant, he distanced himself from the movement. His heart was filled with guilt and confusion, but for his family and future, he believed it was the right choice.

Agent Williams' operation had an impact on every corner of the city. He knew the protests weren't just voices; they were symbols of hope. By breaking these hopes, he not only weakened those standing against the government but also sent a message that every voice could be silenced.

In the operation room, the screens now displayed only blue dots—peaceful and inert. One team member remarked, "Sir, we've crushed the protests."

Williams replied with a faint smile, "The fight isn't over. This is just the beginning. Now we must ensure that no one dares to rise again."

He knew this victory was temporary. People might stay silent, but the spark within their hearts could ignite a new fire at any moment. And he was always ready to extinguish that fire.

An Unseen Future

The city skies were clouded once again. Every household carried its own story—Elena was still fighting for her brother's truth, Kevin had sacrificed his dreams, and the rest watched the struggle in silence.

But somewhere, in a hidden corner, a new plan was brewing. Those who had given up were still questioning within themselves: "Is this truly the end, or is it the sign of a new beginning?"

This struggle wasn't over. It was only a matter of time before another Elena or Kevin gathered the courage to raise their voice.

"The truth can be suppressed, but it can never be erased forever." And the truth is yet to come to light..

10

The Revolt

On a crisp morning, Agent Williams entered the grand municipal building, carrying a bouquet of vibrant flowers that stood out against the gray city hall. With a polite nod to security, he passed the bouquet through the scanner, unaware of the fly-like robotic insect silently slipping into the petals.

Inside, Mayor Greg Davis, energized by his vision for Aurorium's future, returned to his office, eager to enact a transformative law. His secretary announced Williams, who stepped in with the bouquet.

"Congratulations, Mr. Mayor," Williams said smoothly, handing over the flowers.

"Thank you," Davis replied, placing them on his desk. "This law marks a new beginning—a step towards order and progress."

Williams nodded with quiet resolve. "Aurorium is in good hands, sir."

Encouraged by the affirmation, the mayor leaned in slightly, his voice dropping to a conspiratorial tone. "I will make sure the people of this city follow my lead. There will be no room for dissent, and those who challenge my authority will face consequences. It's the only way to build a prosperous, disciplined society."

Williams' expression remained inscrutable, though a subtle tension flickered in his eyes. "Your resolve is commendable, sir. Aurorium City will thrive under your leadership."

The moment was solemn, charged with the weight of what was to come. "Congratulations again, Mr. Mayor," Williams said, stepping back with a final, respectful nod. "It has been an honor to stand by your side. If I may, I shall take my leave."

The mayor smiled briefly, a rare display of warmth as he escorted Williams to the door. But just as the moment passed, fate intervened in the most brutal of ways.

A sudden, deafening explosion ripped through the air. The bouquet, once a symbol of congratulation, now turned into an agent of chaos, detonated with violent force. The blast hurled both men through the shattering door and crumbling wall, their bodies thrown like ragdolls into the midst of the wreckage.

For a moment, time seemed to stand still, the world reduced to a blur of dust and debris. The once-proud office was now a ruin, filled with the acrid smell of smoke and the echoes of destruction. Williams lay dazed, his mind struggling to piece together the fractured reality around him. The mayor, too, was sprawled amidst the wreckage, his once-confident demeanor shattered in the face of this unexpected and deadly turn of events.

In that instant, everything had changed. The new beginning Mayor Davis had envisioned was reduced to rubble, and the city of Aurorium was left to grapple with the consequences of this violent act.

The once-stalwart mayor's office, a symbol of authority and order, now lay in ruin—a chaotic scene bathed in the harsh strobe of emergency lights. The piercing wails of sirens filled the air as a swarm of cop cars and ambulances converged on the site, their presence a grim testament to the violence that had shattered the morning calm. Yellow tape flapped in the wind, cordoning off the emergency zone, where paramedics and firefighters scrambled to treat the wounded and clear the debris.

Amid the frenzied activity, Mayor Greg Davis was gingerly loaded onto a stretcher, his face pale and ashen. The confident resolve that had once marked his every action was now replaced with a glaze of shock, his eyes wide with the dawning realization of how close he had come to death. Blood trickled down his temple, mingling with the dust that clung to his sweat-soaked skin.

As the paramedics prepared to lift him into the ambulance, the mayor's phone vibrated in his pocket. With trembling fingers, he reached for it, his heart pounding with a growing sense of dread. The screen flickered to life, revealing a text message that sliced through the chaos like a knife: "*Your new beginning will come to an end soon.*"

A cold shiver ran down the mayor's spine, the words searing themselves into his mind. Panic surged through him, raw and uncontrollable. His breath quickened, coming in ragged gasps as the reality of the threat hit him like a sledgehammer. He bolted upright, thrashing against the restraints on the stretcher, his voice hoarse as he screamed, "I can't go back in there! I won't set foot in that office again!"

His outburst caught the attention of the nearby responders, who exchanged worried glances. The boundaries of power and safety, once so clearly defined, were now as shattered as the walls of his office. The mayor's previous air of invincibility crumbled, leaving him teetering on the precipice of uncertainty and fear.

The scene around him blurred, the flashing lights and the shouts of emergency personnel fading into a cacophony of terror in his mind. The mayor, who had once stood as a beacon of leadership and control, was now just another frightened man, overwhelmed by the magnitude of the threat that loomed over him. In that moment, he was no longer the master of his own destiny; he was a pawn, trapped in a deadly game with an unseen enemy who had already made the first move.

As the ambulance doors slammed shut and the vehicle sped away, the mayor could do nothing but stare blankly at the message on his phone, his mind reeling with the chilling realization that his 'new beginning' might very well be the beginning of the end.

In a room suffused with the palpable weight of impending danger, government officials gathered once more, their faces etched with the stress of confronting a terror that lurked just beyond their grasp. The air was thick with tension, every word exchanged charged with the urgency of the moment, as they debated how to shield the city from an unseen, intelligent threat.

Agent Williams, his face marred with fresh wounds—a stark reminder of the recent assault—sat silently, absorbing the torrent of suggestions that filled the room. His eyes, sharp and discerning, missed nothing as he listened to the frantic discourse. When the clamor reached its zenith, he raised his hand—a subtle gesture that commanded immediate attention.

"We're not dealing with an ordinary rebel group," Agent Williams began, his voice steady yet laced with a gravitas that cut through the noise. "We don't yet know whether this is the work of an individual or an organized faction. What we do know is that this adversary is methodical and shrewd.

If we act without fully understanding their motives, we risk playing right into their hands."

The room fell into a hushed silence, every eye fixed on the seasoned agent. His words carried the weight of experience, and the officials sensed that what he was about to propose would be far from conventional.

"My suggestion," Williams continued, his tone measured, "is to temporarily halt the implementation of the Child Planning law. This isn't about capitulating; it's about buying time. Time to gather intelligence, to dissect their actions, and to understand the full scope of their intentions."

A ripple of unease swept through the room, the officials shifting uncomfortably as the gravity of the proposal settled in. One, his voice tinged with skepticism, dared to question, "Isn't this just surrendering to terrorists? A sign of weakness?"

Agent Williams met the challenge head-on, his gaze unwavering. "Yes," he replied, his voice unwavering. "It's a calculated retreat. A pause to catch our breath, to learn who we're dealing with. And when we do, we won't just react—we'll strike back with a force so decisive that it will obliterate this threat and serve as a stark warning to any who dare challenge the government."

A heavy silence enveloped the room as the officials grappled with the implications of Williams' strategy. The air buzzed with the tension of a choice that felt like betrayal but was steeped in survival—a paradox of surrender as a prelude to an even greater fight.

As the daylight broke over the city, still shrouded in the aftermath of terror, Mayor Greg Davis, a man now steeled by resolve, summoned the press. The air was electric with anticipation as reporters gathered, sensing that the day would bring news of consequence.

With the full weight of leadership resting on his shoulders, Mayor Davis stepped to the podium. His voice, firm and unyielding, echoed through the room, "Effective immediately, the implementation of the new Child Planning law will be suspended. We must take this time to thoroughly examine its impact, ensuring that every decision we make is for the greater good of our citizens."

The press corps buzzed with questions, cameras flashing as reporters jockeyed for attention. One journalist, his voice sharp with curiosity, pressed, "Is this decision influenced by the recent attack on your office, Mr. Mayor?"

The mayor stood his ground, his eyes narrowing slightly as he dismissed the suggestion with a wave of his hand. "This decision is not driven by fear. It is a measured response, a commitment to our duty as public servants. We will not be cowed by those who seek to disrupt our work."

Undeterred, another voice called out, probing for details on the government's next move against the terror threat. The mayor, his expression one of practiced composure, replied with calculated calm, "The investigation is ongoing. We will update the public as more information becomes available. Rest assured, we are unwavering in our pursuit of justice."

The press conference concluded, leaving behind a throng of reporters with unanswered questions and the city with a decision that hung like a cloud over its future.

In the shadows of power, away from the relentless gaze of the media, Mayor Davis found himself in a quiet corner of his office, seeking the counsel of Agent Williams. The conversation that followed was tense, whispered, and fraught with the gravity of the situation. "Is it safe for me to continue my duties?" the mayor asked, his voice betraying a rare glimpse of vulnerability.

Agent Williams, ever the pillar of resolve, responded with a calm that belied the turmoil they faced. "They've achieved their goal—a temporary pause. For now, they won't strike again. Their objective isn't your life; it's to instill fear, to remind us of their presence. But make no mistake, we'll use this reprieve to dig deep, to understand them. And when the time is right, we'll strike back with everything we have."

Williams' vow echoed like a battle cry, a promise of retribution that would not only withstand the storm but harness its fury when the moment was ripe.

11

The Investigation

Agent Williams stood by the large window of his dimly lit office, the city below sprawling like a living organism, oblivious to the creeping darkness. The fading afternoon light cast long shadows as he drew deeply from his cigar, the smoke curling upwards, as scattered as his thoughts.

Hurried footsteps echoed outside, pulling his attention to the door. It swung open, revealing Agent Morales, her face tense. "Williams," she began, holding out a folder. "Dr. Turner's postmortem on the Mayor. You need to see this."

Taking the folder, Williams scanned its contents. His jaw tightened as the grim details settled in. Moments later, he strode into the lab, the sterile hum of equipment enveloping him. Dr. Emily Turner looked up, urgency replacing her usual calm.

Without a word, she activated a hologram of the Mayor's body, every detail illuminated with haunting precision. "This isn't just a poison," she began, isolating a glowing thread in the holographic bloodstream. "It's a neurotoxin— engineered to attack the central nervous system with ruthless efficiency."

Williams' eyes darkened. "I've never seen anything like this."

"That's because it's not just any neurotoxin," Dr. Emily continued, her tone dropping as if she were revealing a dark secret. "This toxin was extracted from a plant species that was believed to have gone extinct over a century ago—Cyprium Asphyxium."

Williams tilted his head slightly, the name unfamiliar. "Cyprium Asphyxium? "

"Most haven't," Dr. Emily said with a slight nod. "It was a rare and highly dangerous plant, known in ancient texts for its use in ritual poisonings and assassinations. The plant's neurotoxin was potent—capable of shutting down the nervous system slowly. It was said that even the smallest trace could paralyze a person, leaving them alive but unable to move, their mind trapped in a prison of their own body until death mercifully took them."

The room seemed to grow colder as Dr. Emily spoke, the weight of her words pressing down on Williams. His heart pounded in his chest as he realized the magnitude of what she was saying. "But how is it possible that someone…?"

Dr. Emily's expression was grim as she turned back to the hologram, her fingers manipulating the image to highlight the molecular structure of the toxin. "That's what makes this so disturbing. The plant is supposed to be extinct—yet here we are. The fact that this toxin exists means that someone, somewhere, has either found a hidden source of the plant or, more likely, has managed to recreate it synthetically using ancient botanical records. This isn't just a murder, Agent Williams. This is the work of someone who possesses a profound knowledge of both ancient poisons and cutting-edge biochemical engineering."

Williams clenched his fists, the muscles in his jaw tightening as the implications sank in.

Dr. Emily confirmed, her eyes reflecting the gravity of the situation. "This is not the work of a common assassin. Whoever did this is playing a very dangerous game—one that goes beyond what we can even comprehend right now."

Williams let out a slow breath, his mind racing with possibilities. "And this toxin… there's no antidote?"

Dr. Emily shook her head slowly, her expression one of solemn resignation. "None. The toxin is too rare, too complex. Once it's in the bloodstream, it's only a matter of time. The Mayor… he never stood a chance."

A heavy silence fell between them, the weight of the revelation almost too much to bear. Williams stared at the hologram, the image of the Mayor's lifeless body now taking on a more sinister, tragic air. This was no ordinary case. This was something far more dangerous, far more personal. The stakes had just been raised, and he knew they were facing an enemy who was not only deadly but also methodical and intelligent.

Williams turned to Dr. Emily, his voice hardening with resolve. "We need to find out who did this—and how. If they've managed to recreate this toxin, then they've just declared war. And I intend to win it."

Dr. Emily nodded, her own resolve mirrored in Williams' eyes. The battle lines had been drawn, and they both knew there was no turning back. This was just the beginning.

Agent Williams stormed into the high-tech control room, his expression a mask of steely resolve. The revelation from Dr. Emily gnawed at his thoughts like a relentless predator, pushing him to action. He could feel the answers slipping through his fingers, and he was determined to catch them before they vanished into the shadows.

"Get me all the surveillance footage around the Mayor's office on the day of the press conference—every angle, every second," he barked, his voice cutting through the hum of electronics. The tech team sprang into action, fingers flying over keyboards, and the vast screen before them flickered to life, illuminating the room with a mosaic of digital feeds.

Williams leaned in, his eyes narrowed as he scrutinized the footage. Each frame was a potential clue, each second a chance to untangle the web surrounding the Mayor's assassination. Suddenly, his gaze locked onto a particular clip—a woman, seated in a car, her face partially obscured but enough to stir something in his gut.

"Zoom in on that car," he commanded, not tearing his eyes away from the screen. "Enhance the footage—I want to see her face."

The techs worked quickly, the image sharpening until the woman's features came into focus. Williams felt his pulse quicken. She was no ordinary bystander.

"We need more angles," he muttered, more to himself than to the team. "Pull footage from nearby stores, traffic cams, anything."

The room buzzed with activity, screens flickering as they accessed additional feeds. Piece by piece, a clearer picture emerged—a puzzle beginning to take shape.

"Run the plate," Williams ordered, his voice low but firm. "I want every scrap of information on that car. Let's find out who she is."

Within minutes, the data flowed in, and with it, a revelation that sent a jolt of shock through Williams' body. The woman was Elena Rodriguez. The name hit him like a sledgehammer. Elena Rodriguez? How could she be involved?

He didn't waste a second. "Mobilize all units," he snapped, urgency edging his tone. "We need to find her—now."

But Elena was a ghost, slipping away into the city's labyrinthine depths, leaving nothing but questions in her wake. Williams clenched his fists, frustration simmering beneath his calm exterior. He wasn't about to let her get away.

Back in the surveillance room, Williams retraced her every move on the day of the mass protest held at the downtown. The screens flickered as he navigated through a tangle of camera feeds, his focus razor-sharp.

"Enhance that feed," he instructed, leaning over the console, his eyes boring into the shadowy figure on the screen. The image sharpened, revealing Elena in a final moment before she vanished from the cameras' watchful gaze.

His heart pounded as the footage led him to Elena's home—her last known location. Beyond that, nothing. No sign of her leaving. The surveillance feeds, usually so reliable, offered nothing but a black hole where Elena should have been.

Williams muttered under his breath, tension coiling in his chest. "This is where the game changes."

Determined, he delved deeper into the case against Elena's brother, uncovering layers of deception that only deepened the mystery. The woman who filed the charges was missing—vanished, just like Elena. But the more Williams dug, the clearer it became that she wasn't who they thought she was. She wasn't the operative meant to frame Elena's brother. This was something else—something bigger.

He shifted gears swiftly, his mind racing with possibilities. "Find her," he ordered his team. "We trace the missing woman. We dig until we find the link."

But as they followed the trail, it too ended abruptly at the woman's home. Just like Elena, she had disappeared without a trace, leaving behind an empty shell of a life.

Williams' mind spun, but his determination only hardened. Two women, same pattern. He wasn't chasing ghosts; he was chasing something much darker, much more calculated.

Then, the puzzle pieces began to fall into place. The Rodriguez Clinic. Both women had ties to it, a connection that sent a chill down Williams' spine. He couldn't shake the feeling that the clinic was the key to unlocking this tangled conspiracy.

His eyes narrowed, the intensity of his focus unyielding. "Let's crack this wide open," he muttered, his voice laced with the quiet fury of a man who wouldn't stop until the truth was laid bare. And as the investigation plunged deeper into darkness, Williams knew one thing for certain—he was closer than ever to unraveling a mystery that had already cost lives and threatened to claim many more.

12

The Rodriguez Clinic

Agent Williams leaned over the cluttered desk in the surveillance room, his eyes narrowing at the Rodriguez Clinic records scattered before him. The soft glow of multiple screens cast long shadows across the room. His brow furrowed in concentration, his fingers drumming rhythmically on the desk—a sign of the frustration simmering just beneath the surface.

"These women… they all had regular post-pregnancy check-ups," Williams murmured to himself, piecing together the threads of the mystery that had been eluding him. But there was something off—something that didn't add up. He traced the paths of the women in question, their prenatal care, their deliveries. The hospital records offered clinical details, yet the surveillance footage yielded nothing. It was as though these women had never set foot in the hospitals at all.

Agent Williams straightened, his mind racing, determination hardening his resolve. He picked up his comm and barked into it, "Reynolds, I need you in here, now."

Moments later, Agent Reynolds appeared, the door sliding shut behind him with a soft hiss. Williams didn't waste a moment, thrusting the files into his hands. "Interview the gynecologists at every hospital these women supposedly visited. I want to know why none of the doctors remember them."

Reynolds nodded, his expression a mixture of curiosity and concern.

"Understood, sir. But… what if they really did slip through the cracks?"

Williams's gaze was icy, his voice a low growl. "They didn't slip through anything. We're missing something, and I intend to find out what."

Hours later, as the agents reconvened, the mood in the room had darkened. Reynolds returned, shaking his head in frustration. "None of the gynecologists recall seeing these women as patients. It's as if they never existed."

The words hung in the air, adding to the oppressive weight already pressing down on the room. Agent Williams remained unmoved, though his jaw clenched slightly—a sign of the quiet storm brewing within him. "This isn't over," he said, more to himself than anyone else.

He turned sharply toward the surveillance screens, his mind racing as he sought the next move.

Williams's eyes flicked to the screen displaying Dr. Evan's file, the man's face staring back at him impassively. Without missing a beat, Williams barked orders. "Release Dr. Evan. Drop the charges immediately. We're not interrogating him."

Agent Reynolds blinked in surprise, hesitating for a moment before speaking. "But sir, he could have information on Elena's activities. Isn't this our best shot at getting closer?"

Williams turned to face him, his gaze sharp and unyielding. "No. The case is on shaky ground, and the last thing we need is to tip our hand. The complainant's disappearance changes everything. We're not in the business of creating more problems for ourselves."

Morales, leaning against a console, voiced the concern on everyone's mind. "But what if Dr. Evan's involved, sir? We might lose a critical lead."

Williams exhaled slowly, his expression never wavering. "We won't lose anything. We'll keep him under surveillance, no direct contact. If he's involved, he'll slip up, and we'll be there when he does. Until then, we play it smart."

The room seemed to vibrate with the tension of the decision, the unspoken anxieties of the agents around him hanging in the air like a dense fog.

Williams watched as his team dispersed, each agent moving with a sense of purpose but also unease.

He remained standing, staring at the screens with a look of steely resolve. The path to the truth was winding, treacherous, and filled with shadows. But Williams knew, with a certainty that settled deep in his bones, that he was inching closer. Every decision, every move, had to be executed with precision. There was no room for error. The lives of those missing women—and the truth behind their disappearances—depended on it.

And Agent Williams would stop at nothing to unravel the enigma before him.

After his release from the police station, Dr. Evan felt the cold air cling to his skin as he stepped into the medical store. The soft hum of fluorescent lights above contrasted with the heavy weight of his thoughts. He moved down the aisles with a sense of urgency but found himself pausing, uncertain. The layout was different. Everything seemed slightly off, much like his current situation.

As he scanned the shelves, his gaze darted from label to label, trying to make sense of the reorganization. A faint unease crept up his spine. Where were the medical-grade bandages? He'd bought them from this store a dozen times before, yet now, they seemed to have vanished.

"Lost, are we?" The soft voice pulled him from his thoughts. Dr. Evan turned, his eyes meeting the pleasant face of a woman, her smile wide and inviting. Yet, something about her gaze felt too intent, too observing.

He forced a polite smile. "Yes... I usually find medical-grade bandages here, but..."

She tilted her head slightly, her eyes flicking over him in a way that made the hairs on the back of his neck prickle. "They're on the top shelf toward the back," she said, gesturing casually in the direction. "They rearranged some sections recently—trying to fit in more products, you know."

Dr. Evan nodded, his gratitude sincere despite the gnawing suspicion at the back of his mind. "Thank you. I appreciate the help."

The woman's smile lingered, warm but lingering a second too long. "Not a problem at all. Used to work here, actually... until a few days ago." Her voice was light, almost too light, as if she was trying to downplay something.

"Really?" Dr. Evan responded with a touch of curiosity. "Well, thanks again." He offered her a polite nod and turned away, walking toward the back of the store. But as he moved, he felt the weight of her gaze following him—a sensation that stuck with him long after he reached the bandages.

Without turning around, he could sense it—the woman hadn't moved. She was still watching him. Why?

After a moment, he glanced back. But she was gone, slipping away into the aisles like a ghost. The unease that had taken root earlier only deepened, and he couldn't shake the feeling that their encounter had been more than a simple act of kindness.

As he pocketed the bandages and made his way out of the store, Dr. Evan's thoughts churned. Was she just another stranger, or was she connected to the tangled mess he found himself in?

The answer, he feared, might not be so simple.

A few days later, Dr. Evan stepped away from the clinic's busy front desk, his eyes scanning the lobby. Among the applicants for an interview, he spotted a familiar face—Ruth, the woman from the medical store. Their eyes met, and she smiled knowingly.

"Hi, so we meet again," she said warmly.

Dr. Evan, momentarily surprised, replied, "Good to see you again," as he found her resume. "Ruth Moore?"

"That's me," she said confidently, shaking his hand.

In the interview, Ruth's impressive credentials and composure stood out. To test her further, Dr. Evan brought her to a simulation room where a humanoid patient robot greeted her: "Hello, I'm Corey Wilburn. I've been feeling fatigued and having headaches."

Without hesitation, Ruth replied with calm professionalism, "Hello, Mr. Wilburn. I'm Ruth. Let's discuss your symptoms further."

Her interaction was fluid, almost as if she had forgotten the "patient" was just a machine. She gathered information with precision, asking about the robot's medical history, lifestyle, and symptoms with the practiced ease of a seasoned professional. But it wasn't until the robot dramatically clutched its chest and collapsed that the real test began.

For a split second, time seemed to freeze. Dr. Evan watched closely, his breath held in anticipation. Ruth sprang into action without hesitation. Her voice cut through the air, sharp and commanding. "Code Blue! Nurse, get help—now!"

She began CPR, her movements swift and methodical, as if every beat of the robot's heart depended on her. The simulation played out in a tense choreography of life-saving procedures—defibrillators, medication, teamwork. Dr. Evan didn't just observe her medical skills; he saw her leadership, her ability to rally the team and make quick, decisive calls.

When the exercise finally ended, Dr. Evan approached her with measured approval. "Handling a medical emergency isn't just about skill—it's about leadership, about keeping a clear head when everything is on the line. You did well, Ruth."

Her response was calm, as always. "Thank you, Dr. Evan. I'm excited about the opportunity to contribute."

Dr. Evan nodded, more convinced than ever. "I believe you'd be a valuable addition to our team. You start tomorrow. We'll get you acquainted with the procedures and introduce you to the staff."

Ruth smiled, a genuine warmth radiating from her eyes. "I appreciate that, Dr. Evan. I look forward to being a part of the clinic."

But just as they were about to part ways, Ruth's curious nature surfaced. "Dr. Evan, I have to ask—why hire me, a human, when virtual assistants or humanoids could easily do the job?"

He paused, a contemplative smile tugging at the corners of his mouth. "Ruth, you're the first to ask that. It's simple—people trust people. They need to see someone who can empathize with them, who can listen and respond with genuine understanding. Machines can't do that."

Ruth nodded thoughtfully. "You're right. Machines can replicate a lot, but not the human connection."

The next day, after the last patient had left, Ruth lingered in the clinic, her eyes tracing the quiet space. She approached Dr. Evan, who was absorbed in paperwork, his expression focused yet relaxed.

"Dr. Evan," she began, her voice steady but carrying an undercurrent of emotion, "I've been meaning to tell you something."

He looked up, meeting her gaze with an inviting smile. "What's on your mind, Ruth?"

She hesitated for just a moment, then pressed on. "I've been observing you.

The way you run this clinic, your dedication to the community—it's inspiring."

Dr. Evan's smile softened. "Thank you, Ruth. It's what drives me—making healthcare accessible to everyone."

"But it's more than that," she insisted. "You're not just treating patients; you're making a real difference in their lives."

He nodded, the weight of her words sinking in. "It's a team effort, Ruth. And now, you're part of that team."

Ruth smiled, a sense of fulfillment washing over her. But there was more she needed to share. "Dr. Evan," she said, her voice growing more serious, "there's something I need to tell you about my brother..."

She recounted the painful story of her brother's denial of medical care due to the government's heartless social scoring system. Dr. Evan listened intently, his own past struggles with the system surfacing in his mind. Their shared disappointment with the injustices they'd both witnessed formed a bond, solidifying their shared commitment to fight for what was right, both inside and outside the clinic.

The narrative of the day took an unexpected twist when a patient, Julian, arrived with a pregnant friend. Ruth's instincts buzzed, sensing something off. Julian was there for a check-up, but her friend's presence seemed to carry a hidden weight. Ruth discreetly observed the woman, her mind churning with suspicion. As they left, she took a quick photo, sending it to an undisclosed contact with a simple, urgent request: "Follow her. Find out more."

Little did Dr. Evan know, Ruth's journey at the clinic was just beginning, and the secrets she harbored might soon collide with the life they were trying to build together.

13
The Escape

Agent Williams stood in the dimly lit tech control room, the glow of monitors casting shifting shadows across his stern features. The room was a labyrinth of screens, and gadgets—each one tuned to capture every nuance of the investigation at hand.

An Analyst hurried over to Williams, his expression a mix of anxiety and determination. He brought up Jann and Chloe's images on the big screen.

"Sir, I've got something on Jann and Chloe," Analyst's voice steady but laced with urgency. "They're originally from Nebula Vista. Been living here in Aurorium for the last 6 months, though."

Williams turned, his gaze locking onto Daniels with the intensity of someone who'd seen too much but wasn't ready to miss a thing. He nodded slightly, a signal to continue.

"She and her husband Jann relocated to the city, living at their friend's home - Julian. They were looking for a fresh start. At first glance, they're a normal, middle-class couple. No criminal history, no red flags."

"But here's where it gets interesting," Daniels added, his voice dropping slightly as if what he was about to say carried more weight. "Chloe's pregnant. Her due date's not far off."

The control room hummed with life, its walls lined with screens projecting flickering images from various cameras across the city. Agent Williams sat at the helm, his sharp eyes fixed on the largest screen, where a live feed from Chloe's apartment streamed. His fingers drummed on the armrest, a subtle rhythm betraying the tension gnawing at his mind.

On the screen, Chloe moved through her apartment with an unsettling ease. Her husband, Jann, and their friend—Julian were engaged in what appeared to be mundane conversation. But Williams knew better. His instincts, honed by years of chasing shadows, whispered that something more sinister was at play.

"Keep a close watch," Williams muttered, his voice low but laced with authority. "Don't miss a single detail."

Agent Reynolds, stationed in a nearby coffee shop, acknowledged the command with a curt nod. His eyes never left the monitor as he zoomed in on Chloe's expression, trying to decipher the emotions hidden behind her calm facade. Was she aware of the invisible eyes trailing her every move? Or was she simply a pawn in a much larger game?

As nightfall draped the city in darkness, the atmosphere inside Chloe's apartment shifted. Julian gathered her things, preparing to leave. The camera captured the polite exchanges between her and Chloe— pleasantries that felt too practiced, too rehearsed. Reynolds adjusted the camera angle, trying to glean anything from their body language.

Williams leaned forward in his chair, narrowing his gaze at the screen. The unease that had been simmering beneath the surface now flared into full- blown suspicion. There was something in Chloe's eyes—a fleeting glimmer that set off alarms in his mind.

As Julian exited the apartment, Chloe and Jann retreated to their bedroom. The door closed with a soft, ominous creak, and the lights went out, plunging the room into shadow. Williams watched, every muscle in his body coiled with tension.

Minutes ticked by, each one a torturous stretch of silence. The glow of the city outside the apartment barely penetrated the thick curtains, casting faint patterns of light on the walls. Inside the control room, the quiet hum of electronic equipment became deafening in the stillness.

Then, without warning, Williams felt it—an instinctual tug at the back of his mind. Something was wrong. His fingers clenched the armrest, his eyes narrowing in suspicion.

"Go in," he ordered, his voice sharp. "Check the place. Something doesn't feel right."

The field agent moved swiftly, donning night vision glasses before slipping into the building. Outside, the drones maintained their silent vigil, circling the apartment complex like watchful predators. Inside, the agent advanced with the stealth of a shadow, barely disturbing the air around him as he glided through the living room.

As he approached the bedroom door, his heart pounded in his ears. He hesitated, his hand hovering over the handle before finally pushing it open. The room lay in darkness, the bed undisturbed. But Chloe and Jann were gone.

The agent's pulse quickened as he swept the room with his gaze. There were no signs of struggle, no clues left behind. It was as if the couple had vanished into thin air. Panic threatened to claw its way up his throat, but he pushed it down, forcing himself to remain calm.

"Sir," the agent's voice crackled through the earpiece, laced with unease. "They're not here. The room's empty. No sign of them."

In the control room, Williams' jaw clenched. His eyes darted across the monitors, his mind racing through the possibilities. How could they disappear without a trace? His fingers flew over the keyboard, issuing a series of commands.

"Scan the entire building," he barked, his voice tight with urgency. "They can't have gone far. Find them!"

The control room erupted into a flurry of activity as agents scrambled to execute the orders. Drones zipped through the night, their sensors scanning every inch of the building with precision. But the clock was ticking, and with each passing second, the chances of finding Chloe and Jann diminished.

Williams' gaze remained locked on the screen, his thoughts a whirlwind of suspicion and strategy. The night had taken an unexpected turn, plunging him and his team into a web of mystery that seemed to grow darker with every twist. Chloe's disappearance wasn't just a missing persons case—it was a riddle, one that threatened to unravel everything they thought they knew.

And somewhere, in the heart of the city, Chloe and Jann were slipping further out of reach.

Amid the city's pulsating rhythms, Julian maneuvered her car into the Fairmount local station's parking lot. She parked with mechanical precision, her mind elsewhere, heavy with the gravity of her purpose. As she reached into the backseat, pulling out bags, she left the car door ajar—an unfinished act, as if she hadn't fully committed to what was coming next. The trunk popped open with a quiet click, revealing more luggage. After loading up, she slammed it shut and walked away, her stride filled with quiet determination.

Nearby, another vehicle glided to a halt. A man emerged, pulling a suitcase from the trunk, while a woman gracefully stepped out of the passenger seat. The door remained open, a silent testament to the moment they were about to leave behind. They shared a brief kiss—hesitant, tender—before she took her luggage and walked away, leaving the door wide open. The man lingered for a moment, then closed the door gently, as though sealing off that chapter, and slipped into the driver's seat. The car hummed as it merged into the city's night, disappearing as the taillights faded into the distance.

Julian moved through the station with purpose, her eyes scanning the area, always on alert yet never lingering long enough to draw attention. She bought her ticket swiftly, her actions fluid, rehearsed. But beneath her calm exterior, there was a tension—a slight quickening of her pace, a sideways glance that gave away the undercurrent of fear. Unseen by her, agents, shrouded in the shadowy corners of the station, tracked her every move with hawk-like precision. As she boarded the commuter train, she slipped into the crowd, her presence swallowed by the sea of faces, just another nameless figure lost in the city's relentless churn.

Meanwhile, the man who had parted ways with the woman arrived at an isolated, desolate place. His car rolled to a stop at the edge of an abandoned building, half-eaten by the shadows of the night. Dim streetlights barely fought against the darkness, casting long, sinister shadows. He stepped out, leaving the car door wide open, the echo of Julian's actions a haunting mirror image. The man lit a cigarette, taking a long drag as he surveyed the surroundings. The smoke curled around him, merging with the fog that clung to the ground like a specter.

A faint sound broke the eerie silence—a fence rattling in the distance, carried by the wind. The man stiffened, his eyes darting to the source, but the darkness swallowed the noise before he could place it. For a long moment, he remained still, his ears straining for any further disturbance. Then, satisfied—or perhaps resigned—he tossed the cigarette onto the cracked pavement, its embers hissing out as it met the damp ground. He got back into his car, and with a low growl from the engine, the vehicle disappeared into the void.

Behind him, deep within the abandoned building, an ephemeral flash of light flickered—brief, electric—before dying out, leaving the shadows to reclaim their domain once more.

14

The Family Ties

The clinic was quiet, the day winding down, and the soft hum of the lights overhead cast a gentle glow over the room. Dr. Evan Rodriguez and Ruth found a moment of calm, a rare reprieve from their usual routines. In the stillness, Dr. Evan reached for a bottle of whiskey—a small indulgence, a clandestine celebration reserved for the end of the day.

"Here's to another year," he said, pouring the amber liquid into two glasses, his voice carrying a mix of weariness and gratitude. Ruth raised her glass with a warm smile. "Happy birthday, Dr. Evan," she toasted, her voice light but sincere. "A pleasant surprise indeed."

As they sipped, the whiskey's warmth settled, but Dr. Evan's thoughts seemed to drift elsewhere. His gaze lingered on the shadows dancing in the corners of the room, the weight of unspoken memories pressing in. "I wish my family could be here for this," he murmured, a flicker of melancholy crossing his features. The unspoken events of the past hung in the air like a spectre.

Ruth, ever perceptive, caught the shift in his mood. She leaned forward slightly, her tone gentle. "How about some nostalgia?" she suggested. "Show me your childhood. I'd love to see pictures of your family."

Dr. Evan hesitated, but the idea of sharing something so personal with Ruth felt oddly comforting. He reached for a remote, and with a click, the air before them shimmered. The clinic walls seemed to dissolve as holographic images flickered to life—fragments of his past, frozen in time.

Ruth watched, captivated, as the memories unfolded. Her eyes caught on a photo of a young girl, her curiosity piqued. "Who's this?" she asked softly, her finger tracing the outline of the image.

Dr. Evan's expression softened as he followed her gaze. "That's Elena," he said, the name carrying a tenderness that echoed in his voice. A wistful smile touched his lips, but it quickly faded, replaced by a deeper sadness.

The images continued, each one a window into a world that seemed both familiar and distant. Ruth's attention was drawn to another photo—a different girl, but with a striking resemblance. "And this girl?" she asked, her voice filled with genuine interest.

Dr. Evan paused, the weight of the memory heavy in the silence that followed. "That's Ava," he began, his voice thick with emotion. "My sister Elena...she passed away in a tragic accident. After that, my father...he made a decision. He adopted Ava Parker from a foster care centre, trying to fill the void that Elena left behind."

Ruth's eyes widened, the pieces of the story falling into place. "So, Ava... she's not your biological sister?" she asked, seeking clarity, her heart aching for the complexity of it all.

"No," Dr. Evan replied quietly, his voice barely a whisper. "After Elena died, my father not only adopted Ava, but he gave her Elena's name. Officially, she became Elena Rodriguez. It was his way of preserving her memory... and giving Ava a place in our family."

Ruth's breath caught in her throat, the profoundness of the decision settling in. "That's a heavy burden to carry," she said, her voice filled with empathy. "But also...a profound gesture of love."

Dr. Evan nodded, his eyes clouded with memories. "It was. Ava...she embraced it. She became a part of us, even though the name carried so much weight. She grew into it, made it her own. She even followed in my father's footsteps, pursuing astrophysics just like him."

Ruth smiled softly, the depth of the story resonating with her. "Ava is lucky to have found such a caring family," she said gently. "And you've been there for her every step of the way."

Dr. Evan's gaze returned to the holographic images, his eyes tracing the familiar faces. "We're all connected by something deeper than blood," he mused quietly. "It's the choices we make, the love we give, that bind us."

In the tranquil stillness of the clinic, the weight of family bonds and the enduring strength of the human spirit lingered, weaving a tapestry of memory and resilience that filled the air with unspoken understanding.

Dr. Evan's clinic was quiet, the hum of the equipment fading into the background as he and Ruth shared a rare moment of reflection. The holographic images of his past still flickered in the air, casting soft glows across the room, revealing fragments of a life marked by both love and loss.

"You know," Ruth said after a thoughtful pause, her eyes lingering on an image of Dr. Evan's father—stern yet proud, standing in front of a large observatory dome. "I've always been curious about your father's work. Astrophysics... it sounds fascinating. I'd love to see his lab someday."

Dr. Evan's demeanor shifted almost imperceptibly, but Ruth caught it. The slight stiffening of his shoulders, the way his eyes darkened ever so subtly as they flicked away from hers. It was a change so small that most wouldn't notice it—but Ruth was no ordinary observer. She had been trained to detect the faintest of signals, the tiniest shifts in behavior that often betrayed more than words could say.

"The lab..." Dr. Evan's voice was steady, but there was an underlying tension. He hesitated, as if weighing his words carefully. "It's...not really in a state to be shown off. My father's work was...complicated. He valued his privacy."

Ruth nodded, forcing a smile as she took another sip of her drink, trying to brush off the growing unease. "Of course," she replied casually, though her mind was already racing.

"I understand. But if you ever change your mind, I'd still love to see it. I'm fascinated by all things science."

Dr. Evan smiled tightly but offered no further explanation. The conversation drifted to other topics, but Ruth couldn't shake the feeling that something was off. There was a tension in the air now, one that hadn't been there before—a sense of something being deliberately kept out of reach.

Ruth rushed through the door of her apartment. She moved swiftly, her actions sharp and deliberate as she double-checked the locks on her door, bolted the windows, and yanked the curtains closed. At her small, cluttered desk, Ruth reached for the concealed communication device.

The device hummed to life with a low, ominous buzz, and the holographic screen flickered on, casting ghostly blue light across the darkened room. The connection clicked, and within seconds, the holographic image of Agent Williams materialized before her. His calm, composed figure floated in the centre of her tiny apartment, the glow of the projection giving him an otherworldly presence. Despite the static sheen, his eyes were sharp—ever watchful, ever calculating.

"Ruth," his voice cut through the tension like a blade, low and commanding. No pleasantries, just a name, as if he already knew she bore news that could shake their entire operation.

Her breath hitched, but she wasted no time. "Agent Williams, you were right. Dr. Evan—he's hiding something... something huge. The lab - There's a darker side, and I'm not sure what he's planning, but it's big."

As she spoke, Ruth's eyes never left Williams' face, searching for any sign of emotion. But he remained still, absorbing every word like a sponge, his expression unreadable. When she finished, a heavy silence settled between them, broken only by the faint hum of the device.

Agent Williams finally nodded, his calmness unnerving. "We'll need to tread carefully. Monitor him closely, but don't tip your hand. We need to know exactly what we're dealing with before we make our move."

He paused, his eyes narrowing slightly as if he could see right through her. "And Ruth... be careful. If he's hiding this, there's no telling what lengths he'll go to protect it."

Ruth nodded, her throat tight. "Understood."

With that, Williams' image flickered and dissolved into the air, leaving her alone in the oppressive quiet of her apartment. The silence felt heavier now, filled with the gravity of the mission ahead. Her heart pounded against her ribs as she leaned back in her chair, the enormity of what she'd discovered finally crashing down on her.

She closed her eyes, letting the darkness of the room envelop her. There was no turning back now. Every step forward would be a step into the unknown, a step closer to whatever truth lay buried in Dr. Evan Rodriguez's shadowy world. And whatever it was, Ruth knew it would change everything.

15

The Sinister Deeds

In the heart of a sprawling, high-tech laboratory hidden deep within a fortress of secrecy, the soft hum of machinery reverberated through the air. This wasn't just any research facility—it was a breeding ground for moral corruption. Rows upon rows of sleek, cylindrical incubators filled the expansive room, each one cradling a tiny, sleeping infant. The setup resembled a massive beehive, but instead of honey, it produced life—innocent life, engineered and nurtured for a sinister purpose.

The incubators, glowing with a pale, sterile light, hummed with a soft vibration that mimicked the soothing rhythms of a womb. Inside, the infants lay motionless, their tiny forms bathed in an artificial warmth, oblivious to the dark intentions that buzzed around them. Medical professionals, clad in pristine white lab coats, glided silently between the rows, their expressions masked by the cold, calculated detachment of science. To them, these children were not human beings, but variables in a grand experiment.

Yet, the true horror of this lab was not confined to its walls.

In a hidden chamber far removed from the sterile environment of the lab, power and greed mingled with the scent of old money and corruption. An opulent room, adorned with priceless art and plush furnishings, served as the clandestine meeting place for the powerful and the corrupt. Here, under the dim glow of chandeliers, politicians and businessmen—unscrupulous souls driven by insatiable greed—convened for a vile transaction that blurred the lines between science and inhumanity.

The air was thick with secrecy as masked buyers from across the globe gathered in the shadows, their identities obscured but their intentions unmistakably vile. They had not come for art or artifacts, but for something far more grotesque: children. The auction was no ordinary sale; it was a bidding war for the futures of these innocent souls.

The centerpiece of this twisted spectacle was a cutting-edge predictive modeling system, a chilling display of technological prowess developed by the very scientists who now stood behind the veil of ethics. This system, utilizing advanced algorithms and genetic data, projected the future appearance of each infant with eerie accuracy. Not only did it predict how they would look as adults, but it also estimated their potential lifespan—a macabre detail that only added to the allure of the transaction.

As the auction commenced, the lights dimmed, and a large screen illuminated the room. On it, the faces of the infants appeared, side by side with their predicted adult selves—perfect, symmetrical, and unnervingly flawless. The audience watched in silence, their eyes gleaming with desire as they assessed the potential of each child.

The auctioneer, a figure draped in dark charisma, took the stage. His voice, dripping with both reverence and manipulation, echoed through the chamber. "Ladies and gentlemen," he began, his tone a careful blend of persuasion and command, "behold the wonders of modern science! Our revolutionary predictive modeling system offers you a glimpse into the future—an opportunity to invest not just in a child, but in a future of unrivaled beauty, intelligence, and power."

He gestured grandly at the screen, where the infants' projected futures played out like a twisted advertisement. "Imagine," he continued, his voice sinking into the depths of temptation, "the grace, the allure, the brilliance these children will exude as they mature. Today, you do not simply buy a life—you purchase a masterpiece."

In the hushed darkness, the buyers whispered among themselves, their conversations laced with both speculation and greed.

"Look at this one," a man muttered, his gaze fixated on an image of a child predicted to grow into a stunningly symmetrical adult. "Perfect for the fashion industry. That face will sell millions."

"Perhaps," another murmured, "but the intellectual potential here," he pointed to a projected IQ score, "could create a prodigy. A mind that could reshape industries."

"And don't forget entertainment," a third chimed in, eyeing a child with a dazzling future smile. "That charm is destined for the silver screen."

The auctioneer, sensing the rising hunger in the room, pressed on, his voice a sinister thread weaving through their desires. "Remember, you are not merely acquiring a child," he intoned, "you are securing a future—a future of power, of beauty, of influence. Bid wisely, for this is more than a transaction; it is an investment in destiny."

The room buzzed with the energy of the bids that followed, a sickening blend of greed and ambition. On the screen, the infants remained silent, unaware of the monstrous decisions being made about their futures. They were no longer children in the eyes of the buyers—they were commodities, pawns in a grotesque game where their humanity was overshadowed by their predicted allure.

And as the final bids were called and the gavel struck, sealing their fates, the room fell silent once more. In that moment, it was clear: these children, engineered and auctioned off like possessions, were lost to a world that saw them not as innocent lives, but as mere projections—beautiful, marketable, and ultimately expendable.

Across town, in the bustling clinic of Dr. Evan Rodriguez, Ruth, the dedicated assistant, greeted a seemingly ordinary patient named Nick Rogers. But even in the relative normalcy of the clinic, the weight of unseen horrors hung over her. She couldn't shake the feeling that something was amiss—an instinct she had learned to trust over the years.

Ruth: "Hello, sir. How may I help you?"

Nick Rogers: "Hi, I'm Nick Rogers. I scheduled an appointment with Dr. Evan at 4 pm."

Ruth glanced at the appointment screen, her fingers brushing against the cool surface of the desk. "Yes, I see that. Could you please fill out this form for me?"

Nick nodded and took the clipboard, but Ruth couldn't help notice the tension in his hands as he held the pen. Something about him felt off—too guarded, too purposeful. As he filled out the form, she tried to push the unease away, focusing on her work. But when he returned the form, his behavior nagged at her, refusing to be ignored.

Ruth: "Thank you, Nick." She offered a polite smile, but her eyes searched his face, noting the lines of stress etched into his expression. "Is everything alright? You seem tense."

Nick: "No, I'm fine. Thank you." His reply was quick.

As Nick sat in the waiting area, his foot tapped nervously against the floor, his eyes darting toward the door to Dr. Evan's office. Ruth's suspicion deepened. She discreetly checked Nick's appointment history, her heart quickening when she realized he had been here frequently—more often than most patients. And the fact that he was a government employee. It set off alarm bells in her mind.

Why would a government official be visiting their small clinic so often? And why was he so on edge? Something didn't add up.

Ruth's hands trembled slightly as she filled a paper cup with water. The faint sound of the cooler gurgling beneath her fingertips did little to mask the thudding of her heart. She glanced at Nick Rogers, who sat across the room, tapping his foot anxiously against the tile floor. His eyes darted around the clinic, his impatience growing with every passing second.

She swallowed hard, the tiny microphone tucked securely in her palm, its smooth surface cool against her skin. She had to act fast. If she hesitated, she might lose her chance to uncover what Nick was hiding. Every instinct screamed at her that this man was tied to something far more sinister than just a routine appointment.

Ruth had seen enough suspicious behavior in her time at the clinic to know when something wasn't right. But this? This was different. She couldn't let it go, couldn't ignore the gut feeling gnawing at her.

Composing herself, she approached Nick with a warm, practiced smile—the kind that put patients at ease. "Mr. Rogers, you seem a bit tense. Would you like some water while you wait?"

Nick's head snapped up, his eyes meeting hers. For a brief moment, suspicion flickered in his gaze, but then it softened. He nodded, his lips forming a tight smile. "Sure, thanks."

She handed him the cup, her fingers brushing against his as she did. It was a fleeting touch, one that seemed innocent enough. But in that moment, with her heart hammering in her chest, Ruth deftly slipped the tiny microphone onto the inner cuff of his jacket sleeve. The movement was subtle, almost imperceptible—just a practiced flick of her wrist, honed from years of observing the smallest details in the clinic.

Nick took the cup from her, oblivious to the delicate device now nestled against the fabric of his sleeve. Ruth's breath caught in her throat, but she forced herself to stay calm, her expression never faltering. She couldn't afford to let him see through her mask of professionalism.

"Let me know if you need anything else," she said softly, turning away before he could respond.

Ruth returned to the reception desk, her steps measured, each one feeling like it stretched for miles. She could feel the weight of the tiny earpiece hidden in her pocket—an extension of the microphone now attached to Nick. Sliding into her chair, she glanced around the clinic, making sure no one was watching too closely. The room was quiet, the other patients absorbed in their own thoughts, unaware of the high-stakes game unfolding before them.

With a quick, practiced motion, she pulled the earpiece from her pocket and slipped it into her ear, careful to keep her movements subtle. The small device fit snugly, almost invisible beneath her hair. Her heart raced as she adjusted the volume, bracing herself for what she might hear.

A faint crackle buzzed through the earpiece, and then, voices emerged—low and muffled at first, but gradually sharpening as the conversation between Nick and Dr. Evan began to filter through.

Ruth's pulse quickened. Every word that echoed in her ear felt like a thread unraveling, pulling her deeper into a web of deceit she had only begun to glimpse. She focused intently, straining to catch every detail, every inflection in their voices.

Nick's voice came through first, tense and urgent. "Evan, we don't have much time. The project is spiraling out of control."

Ruth's breath hitched. The project. There it was again—mentioned in such a way that confirmed her worst fears. She leaned back in her chair, her eyes fixed on the screen in front of her, but her mind was miles away, locked onto the conversation unfolding in Dr. Evan's office.

Dr. Evan's reply was quieter, more cautious. "What do you mean, Nick? How bad is it?"

Nick's voice lowered, forcing Ruth to strain harder to hear. "Bad enough that we're talking about full-scale cloning operations—genetic manipulation, mind control."

Ruth's blood ran cold. She had suspected something was off, but this... this was far worse than she could have imagined. Her fingers tightened around the edge of the desk, knuckles white with tension.

Ruth's mind raced, each revelation more damning than the last. She had to stay calm, had to process everything without letting her emotions betray her. There was too much at stake now.

As the conversation in Dr. Evan's office grew more intense, Ruth pressed the earpiece closer, her heart pounding in her chest. She knew she was on the brink of something huge—something that could change everything. But with that knowledge came a terrible realization.

She wasn't just an observer anymore. She was a player in this game, whether she wanted to be or not. And the stakes were life and death.

Her pulse thrummed in her ears as she listened to Nick and Dr. Evan's voices continue to unravel the dark conspiracy that had ensnared them all. Each word was a thread, pulling Ruth deeper into a labyrinth of secrets from which there might be no escape.

But she couldn't stop now. She had to know. She had to hear it all.

When Nick finally left, Ruth's mind was a whirlwind of questions and fear. She couldn't keep quiet any longer. Marching into Dr. Evan's office, she confronted him, her voice trembling with a mix of anger and betrayal.

"What was that about, Dr. Evan? What's going on with this project? Are we involved in something we shouldn't be?"

Dr. Evan, his face pale and drawn, met her gaze with a somber expression. He took a deep breath, knowing that there was no turning back now. "Ruth... There's something you need to know."

And with that, the floodgates opened. Dr. Evan revealed the truth behind the project—the twisted experiments, the government's involvement, and the children who were being exploited in the name of science. It was a truth that shattered Ruth's perception of the world, plunging her into a web of intrigue and moral decay that she never thought she'd encounter.

As Dr. Evan detailed the horrors of the project, Ruth felt a cold resolve settle within her. She had always been someone who fought for what was right, and now, she realized that the fight ahead of her was bigger than she ever imagined.

"Dr. Evan," she said, her voice steady despite the turmoil within, "we can't just stand by and let this happen. We have to do something."

Dr. Evan nodded, his eyes heavy with the weight of their shared knowledge. "I know, Ruth. But it won't be easy. The people behind this... They won't stop at anything to protect their secrets."

Ruth's jaw clenched. "Then we'll have to be smarter. We'll find a way to bring them down."

And in that moment, the clinic became something more—a battleground for truth, where the lines between healer and rebel blurred in the face of the corruption they now stood against.

16

The Parallel Universe

As the clinic's lights dimmed and the final echoes of the day's footsteps faded, Dr. Evan swiftly grabbed his invisible coat, his movements precise, urgent. He turned to Ruth, his voice a low whisper, almost swallowed by the silence of the empty halls. "We need to leave now."

Ruth, caught off guard by the sudden shift in his demeanor, raised an eyebrow. "To where?"

A glimmer of secrecy danced in his eyes as he offered her no more than, "You'll see."

Without further explanation, Dr. Evan led her out into the cold night air. They moved with purpose, their footsteps echoing against the cobblestones as they made their way to the station tunnel. The city above them faded away as they descended into the dim-lit underground, the shadows seeming to swallow them whole.

Wrapped in cloaks of invisibility, they wove through the labyrinthine tunnels. The faint hum of distant surveillance cameras served as a constant reminder of the danger they evaded. Ruth's heart raced as they crept deeper into the dank air of the drainage system, the rusted ladder groaning under their weight as they ventured further into the darkness.

Emerging from the belly of the tunnels, they found themselves standing before a decrepit, abandoned building. The wind whispered through broken windows, and an eerie silence hung heavy in the air.

Dr. Evan caught her eye, a wordless understanding passing between them, before they both draped themselves once more in the invisibile cloak and slipped inside.

Once inside, Dr. Evan moved swiftly, peeling back layers of invisibility to reveal what lay hidden beneath—a machine unlike any Ruth had ever seen. It shimmered into existence, casting an otherworldly glow across the dusty room. Ruth's breath caught in her throat, her eyes widening as the scene unfolded before her.

He stepped into the machine, his movements deliberate, before pausing to look back at Ruth, his eyes urging her forward. But Ruth hesitated. Doubt flickered in her gaze, her brow furrowed as she wrestled with the magnitude of the decision before her.

"Ruth. Hurry up," Dr. Evan's voice cut through the silence, pulling her back to the present.

With a deep breath, Ruth stepped forward, the weight of uncertainty still heavy in her chest. She watched as Dr. Evan, composed and methodical, activated the machine. The room hummed to life as a holographic display flickered into existence beneath his fingertips. His hands danced over the keys, and the machine responded with a low, resonant whir.

Then, as if summoned from another realm, a luminous portal materialized before them, its ethereal light casting long shadows across the room. Ruth felt the air shift around her as they moved toward the portal, drawn by its magnetic pull. The world around them blurred as they stepped into the light, and within an instant, the darkness swallowed them whole.

When the obscurity finally lifted, Ruth blinked against the sudden change. They stood in a world that felt both familiar and foreign—a parallel universe, a mirror image of their own yet distinctly different. The air here was electric, tinged with an energy that set Ruth's nerves on edge. She exchanged a glance with Dr. Evan, the unspoken realization hanging between them: their journey into the unknown had only just begun.

As they stepped out of the portal, Ruth's breath caught in her throat at the sight that greeted them. A figure stood waiting, a warm smile lighting up her face—Elena. Dr. Evan's reaction was instant, relief flooding his features as he rushed forward to embrace her. The hug they shared was tight, desperate, as if they had been separated for far too long.

"Are you alright?" Dr. Evan's voice trembled with concern, his hands gripping Elena's shoulders as if to assure himself she was truly there.

Elena's smile widened as she reassured him. "I'm fine. Father is well, too. And Chloe…" her voice softened, "Chloe is about to give birth. Dr. Helen is with her."

Dr. Evan's face lit up with both relief and joy. "That's wonderful news."

Introductions followed quickly as Dr. Evan presented Ruth. Elena, in turn, questioned the state of affairs on their side. But Ruth, still reeling from the sudden shift in reality, could only express her confusion as Elena led them toward a nearby building.

As they walked, the new world unfurled itself before Ruth's eyes. It lacked the cold sophistication of her own, yet there was a charm to it—an unassuming warmth that softened its edges. Here, the pervasive surveillance of her universe was absent. Instead, the streets bustled with life—children playing, elderly couples laughing in cafes, a simpler, kinder world.

But Ruth's bewilderment only grew as they arrived at their destination, where she was confronted with the impossible—a second Elena, an exact replica standing before her. Elena introduced the woman with a knowing smile. "Ruth, meet Dr. Helen. Helen, meet Ruth."

Ruth's mind struggled to comprehend what her eyes were seeing. "She… she looks exactly like you," Ruth stammered. "How…how is that possible?"

Elena's serene smile remained as she began to unravel the mysteries of the multiverse. "Ruth, in this vast cosmos, it's not impossible to encounter someone who looks just like you. But such encounters are rare, given the enormity of it all." She paused, her gaze softening. "I was lucky enough to find my doppelganger. And she turned out to be a wonderful person, just like you."

Ruth fell silent, her thoughts spinning as she tried to make sense of the world she had stepped into. The concept of the multiverse suddenly seemed vast, incomprehensible, yet fascinating.

Amidst the marvels of this new reality, Ruth's curiosity burned brighter than ever. Turning to Elena, she voiced the questions that had been bubbling up inside her. "Who is Chloe? And why is her delivery so important?"

Elena's calm demeanor remained as she began to explain the covert mission that had brought them here. "Chloe is from Ethereal Nexus, the world we come from. She, along with other women, was smuggled to this universe to give birth safely. Our world's oppressive laws put their lives in danger, and we brought them here to protect them."

Ruth struggled to absorb the enormity of the revelation. Ruth's mind refused to rest. "But how did you even find this universe?"

At that moment, another voice cut through the conversation—Dr. Michael Rodriguez, Elena's father, stepping in to fill the gaps. "Our ancestors always sought contact with alien civilizations. After countless attempts, I finally succeeded. That connection led to the creation of the portal. But even now, finding the exact coordinates remains a challenge."

Elena continued, "That's when we found Dr. Helen. Despite knowing we weren't from this world, she chose to trust us. She helped us in ways we never imagined, ensuring the safety of the mothers and their children. Without her, none of this would have been possible."

The weight of their mission hung heavy in the air, the lengths they had gone to protect the vulnerable resonating in the silence that followed.

Ruth felt the pieces of the puzzle begin to click into place. As she gazed out of the window at the unfamiliar cityscape, a final question lingered in her mind. "So, what do you call this place? And what year is it?"

Dr. Helen, with a knowing smile, replied, "This is Earth. You're in St. Louis, Missouri. And the year… is 1965."

Astonishment flickered across Ruth's face as the reality of her situation settled in.

17

The Mole

In a tranquil corner of the Cosmos Universe, Elena watched as Chloe cradled her newborn—a tiny, fragile life swaddled in warmth and love. The scene was a poignant reminder of the delicate beauty that persisted even amid chaos. Chloe's smile, radiant and weary, was a beacon of hope in this distant refuge.

Yet, as Elena gazed at the baby, a quiet unease settled in her chest. This world, for all its peace, was not their home. And home, Aurorium, was a place of danger and oppression. The contrast between this moment of tenderness and the looming reality of their mission gnawed at her.

Jann, Chloe's husband, approached Elena with a hesitant step, his eyes searching hers for answers. "Elena," he began, his voice tinged with anticipation, "any idea when we can head back to Aurorium?"

Elena's gaze lingered on the newborn before she met Jann's eyes. "We have to be patient, Jann. The government has tightened its grip. Surveillance in Aurorium is more intense than ever. It's not safe for us to return just yet."

Her words, though gentle, carried the weight of caution and the burden of leadership. But beneath her calm exterior, a plan was already forming—a plan to return to Ethereal Nexus and the city they called home. The portal, a shimmering gateway between worlds, held both promise and peril. Elena knew that the journey back would be a gamble, one that she and Dr. Evan were willing to take.

When the time came, Dr. Evan, her steadfast companion, prepared the portal with practiced hands. The air hummed with energy as the portal began to glow, casting an otherworldly light across the room. With a shared glance of determination, Elena and Dr. Evan stepped into the swirling vortex, leaving behind the cozy haven of the Cosmos Universe. The cosmic energies enveloped them, and in an instant, they vanished—reclaiming their fate.

Meanwhile, on a quiet street on planet Earth, Ruth and Dr. Michael Rodriguez strolled through a neighborhood bathed in the soft glow of street lamps. The air was crisp, fragrant with blooming flowers, and the distant sounds of children playing echoed through the evening. It was a world apart from the towering skyscrapers and sterile environments of Aurorium.

Ruth marveled at the simplicity of it all. "This is so different from Aurorium," she remarked, her voice tinged with wonder. "No holographic billboards, no oppressive surveillance. It feels… almost unreal."

Dr. Michael nodded, his eyes reflecting a similar appreciation. "Indeed, Ruth. Earth has its charm. The greenery, the gentle hum of nature—it's a stark contrast to the controlled chaos of our city. It reminds us of what we've sacrificed in the name of progress."

As they passed by a small park, the rustling leaves overhead created a soothing melody. Dr. Michael's voice softened with reflection. "Aurorium was built on the principles of efficiency and advancement. But sometimes, I wonder if we've lost something along the way—the simplicity, the closeness to nature."

Ruth nodded, absorbing the serene atmosphere. "There's a certain beauty in this simplicity. Earth has its own rhythm, its own way of being. It makes me think about what we've left behind in our pursuit of progress."

Dr. Michael's gaze drifted to the stars. "Perhaps there's a balance we need to find. Progress is essential, but not at the cost of losing touch with our humanity."

Their conversation wound through the moonlit streets, bridging the gap between two worlds with contrasting ideologies. The calm of the night wrapped around them, but beneath the surface, a tension simmered—an undercurrent of unresolved conflicts.

Ruth's brow furrowed as a new thought emerged. "But the revolt against the government… It doesn't seem to be taking a righteous path. Poisoning the mayor, the protests—it feels more like cruelty than justice. Isn't there a line that shouldn't be crossed?"

Dr. Michael's gaze remained fixed on the path ahead. "Intent is the compass that guides us, Ruth. Sometimes, the course we take is less important than the destination."

"But what if, in our fight for justice, we become what we despise?" Ruth pressed on, her voice laced with concern. "Murdering the mayor—it feels like we're descending into chaos, not rising against tyranny."

Dr. Michael stopped, turning to face her, his expression grave. "Change often emerges from chaos, Ruth. History teaches us that upheaval precedes enlightenment. The actions we take may seem drastic, but they carry the weight of a collective yearning for freedom."

Ruth's mind churned with conflicting thoughts. She understood the desperation that fueled rebellion, but the morality of the means employed gnawed at her.

As they arrived back at their residence, the weight of their differing philosophies hung in the air like an unresolved question. Dr. Michael unlocked the door, but before they could settle in, he turned to Ruth, a sharp glint in his eyes.

"You said something intriguing during our walk, Ruth." She looked at him, curiosity piqued. "What do you mean?"

Dr. Michael's voice lowered, taking on a dangerous edge. "The fact that the Mayor was poisoned wasn't public knowledge. So, I'm wondering—how did you know about it, Agent Karen?"

For a moment, Ruth—no, Agent Karen—stood frozen, her carefully constructed facade cracking. But she quickly regained her composure, her expression hardening. "Well, Dr. Michael, it seems you've uncovered my secret. And now, I have no choice but to protect my cover."

Dr. Michael smiled—a cold, knowing smile. "Fair enough. But remember, I, too, must be prepared."

Karen's gaze sharpened, her voice deadly calm. "Of course. But my focus isn't on you. It's on Elena, as you call her."

Dr. Michael's eyes narrowed, his fatherly instinct flaring. "And yet, you're here with me, not with her."

Karen's lips curled into a smirk. "For now. But soon, you'll take me back, and I'll kill you both—along with your son."

Dr. Michael's voice grew steely. "As a father, I will do everything in my power to protect my children."

Karen's smile widened, her eyes gleaming with menace. "Try me."

Dr. Michael's response was cold and measured. "I already have." A flicker of confusion crossed Karen's face. "What do you mean?"

Dr. Michael's gaze remained steady. "I poisoned your coffee, the same way the Mayor was poisoned. You were so desperate to uncover the secrets about the poison and track down my daughter… But what you didn't know is that your cover was blown the moment you became Dr. Evan's assistant."

Karen's eyes widened as realization dawned, but before she could react, her body betrayed her. Her nails darkened to maroon, her eyes began to bleed, her heart raced uncontrollably. She stumbled, trying to reach Dr. Michael, but her legs gave way. She collapsed at his feet, her breath ragged, her vision blurring.

From the shadows, Dr. Helen emerged, her voice calm and unwavering. "You did the right thing, Dr. Michael. The mole has been removed."

Dr. Michael looked down at Karen's lifeless form, his heart heavy with the weight of his actions. "Yes," he whispered, "but at what cost?"

18

The Hack

As Elena and Dr. Evan returned to Aurorium through the shimmering portal, Elena wasted no time. She activated her tab, sending encrypted messages to the leaders of the resistance. Malik Khan, Olivia Chang, Carlos Gomez, and Kevin Miller all received the coded signals, their resolve hardening. The time had come to reignite their fight against the tyrannical regime.

Elena and Olivia moved swiftly to execute their plan. Their target: Richard Mercer, the government's top official in charge of tech security across Aurorium. The stakes were high, and failure was not an option.

Under the cover of night, they donned their invisible cloaks, slipping into Mercer's vast, fortress-like residence with practiced ease. The halls were eerily silent, safe for the occasional footstep of patrolling guards. The tension was palpable, a cold, sharp thing that cut through the air as they navigated the dimly lit corridors.

In Mercer's room, the soft sound of his breathing filled the space. He lay unaware in his bed, oblivious to the shadows creeping closer. Elena and

Olivia moved like phantoms, their movements synchronized and precise. With a swift motion, Elena injected Mercer with a tranquilizer, ensuring he would remain in a deep, untroubled sleep.

"Quickly, Olivia," Elena whispered, her voice barely audible. "We don't have much time."

Olivia nodded, her hands steady despite the adrenaline coursing through her veins. She opened a sleek case, revealing a small, advanced chip designed for data extraction. With careful hands, Elena placed a chip behind Mercer's ear, the same kind she now affixed behind her own.

The room seemed to pulse with anticipation as Olivia connected wires between the equipment, Mercer, and Elena. The transfer process began, a delicate dance of technology and subterfuge. Outside, the muffled sound of footsteps echoed in the hallway, a stark reminder of the danger that lurked just beyond the door.

"Someone's coming," Olivia whispered, her eyes wide with urgency. "Get under the cloak, now!"

In an instant, they were concealed beneath the invisible fabric, their hearts pounding as the door creaked open. A guard entered, his heavy boots thudding against the floor like a death knell. He scanned the room, suspicion flickering in his eyes.

For a moment, it seemed they were safe, but fate played a cruel trick. The guard stumbled, his foot catching on something unseen—Mercer's leg.

Confusion spread across his face as he tried to regain his balance, his hand reaching out and colliding with the invisible cloak.

"What the hell?" the guard muttered, panic creeping into his voice.

Olivia activated her bracelet that scanned the guard from behind. A lattice of barely visible nanofilaments spread across her body, mapping every contour and dimension. Within seconds, these filaments projected a highly detailed holographic skin over Olivia, transforming her appearance entirely that of the guard.

The guard tugged at the fabric, revealing the shocking sight of Mercer's unconscious form and the figure of Elena poised beside him.

His eyes widened in disbelief, but before he could raise the alarm, Olivia acted with deadly precision. A tranquilizer dart struck him, and he crumpled to the ground in a heap. The room fell back into an eerie silence, the danger momentarily averted.

"Keep going," Elena urged, her voice taut with tension. "We're almost out of time."

The transfer process continued, the equipment humming softly as it extracted the critical data from Mercer's brain. Olivia kept her ear pressed to the guard's communicator, straining to catch any conversation that might hint at their discovery.

Suddenly, a voice crackled through the earpiece. "Report, Peterson."

Olivia's heart raced as she took a deep breath, forcing herself to adopt a casual tone. "Uh, yeah, everything's fine here. Just cleaning my ear."

A pause followed, the silence heavy with uncertainty. Olivia's mind raced, searching for any sign of suspicion.

"Peterson, what took you so long?" Another voice, sharper, more demanding, cut through the static.

"Uh, had to clean my ear, you know?" Olivia replied, her voice faltering slightly. She prayed it was enough.

The second guard grunted, seemingly satisfied with the explanation. "Fine, just hurry up. We need eyes on the hallway."

The moment the second guard left, Olivia exhaled a breath she didn't realize she was holding. The transfer process completed with a soft beep, and Elena's eyes snapped open, the new information glowing in her brain.

"We have what we need," Elena whispered, a determined glint in her eyes. "Let's get out of here."

The following morning, as the sun cast its first light over Aurorium, Richard Mercer—at least, a perfect replica of him—stepped out of his residence.

The car waiting for him started smoothly, the driver none the wiser to the deception unfolding.

Inside the government's intelligence and tech center, the faux Richard moved with purpose. His mannerisms were flawless, indistinguishable from the real Mercer. As he reached the secure tech room, the guards offered no resistance, the familiar face granting him unquestioned access.

In the dimly lit room, he began typing, his fingers moving with a confidence born of the real Mercer's memories. On the other end, Olivia and her tech team watched as the screen illuminated with success.

"Elena, we're in," Olivia's voice crackled over the earpiece, barely able to contain the excitement.

Back at Mercer's residence, chaos erupted. The real Richard and the unconscious guard were discovered in a bathtub, the alarm blaring as security forces mobilized. Within moments, humanoid robots and drones surrounded the tech center, their sensors locked onto the impostor inside.

"Elena, do it now!" Olivia urged, her fingers flying over the keyboard as she directed the rebellion's final move.

The robots, now reprogrammed to distinguish friend from foe, turned on the human guards, neutralizing them with a cold efficiency. In a matter of seconds, the once impenetrable government fortress was brought to its knees.

Throughout Aurorium, government buildings locked down as drones patrolled the skies, ready to engage any who resisted. The rebellion, once a scattered collection of dissidents, had seized control. The city that had long been a symbol of oppression now stood paralyzed, its iron grip shattered by the collective might of Elena's group.

19

The Truth

In the lobby of the government building, the rebels, armed and clad in stealth suits, made their move. The rebels, quick and coordinated, stormed an ancillary room, securing advanced weaponry and flew away in stealth suits.

As they infiltrated the building, Agent Williams, the embodiment of government authority, tried to escape. However, he found himself surrounded by the very rebels he had underestimated. Humanoid Robo cops, now under the rebels' control, seized him, dragged him to a chair, their weapons trained on the once untouchable agent.

While the rebels took strategic positions, Elena, their leader, focused on a different objective. In a secluded area, she feverishly accessed the government's databases, searching for information on the auctions of children and the sinister details of child trafficking. Her intent was clear – to track down the young souls ensnared in this web of corruption and rescue them from the clutches of evil.

As the rebels corralled corrupted government employees in the building's lobby, Elena took centre stage. Her orders were precise: deploy groups to locate and liberate the children who had been sold like commodities. It was a mission driven by a sense of justice that transcended the boundaries of rebellion.

Amidst the orchestrated chaos, Elena descended to the lobby, where Agent Williams, now a captive in his own fortress, awaited judgment. The air was charged with tension as Elena approached him, ready to confront the architect of corruption. The rebel leader's eyes bore into Agent Williams, and in that charged silence, a reckoning awaited – a confrontation that would unveil the depths of corruption and unveil a path towards justice.

Elena, her eyes ablaze with determination, approached the captured Agent Williams in the lobby of the government building. As she walked, the disguise of Richard Mercer gradually faded away magically, revealing Elena. The rebels, still in their stealth suits, stood guard, ensuring that their once powerful captive remained restrained.

Elena: (*coldly*) "Agent Williams, your days of orchestrating the government's dark deeds are over."

Agent Williams: (*smirking*) "You rebels think you can change anything? You're just pawns in a game much bigger than you."

Elena: "We're here to expose the "Council of Shadows" orchestrating the events behind the façade of the Child Planning Law, not to play your games."

Elena: (*fiercely*) "Do you have any idea what you've done? The lives you've ruined, the families torn apart?"

Agent Williams: (*smirking*) "It's for the greater good, Elena. Sacrifices for the progress of society."

Elena: (*scornfully*) "Greater good? Progress? You've become so self-obsessed that you've forgotten the very essence of humanity."

Agent Williams: (*mockingly*) "Humanity? You rebels are naïve. You can't understand the complexities of governance."

Elena: (*with raw emotion*) "Governance? This isn't governance; this is pure evil! You've auctioned off innocent lives like commodities. How can you live with yourself?"

Elena: (*angrily*) "There's no justification for the darkness you've unleashed. You've betrayed your duty, your humanity!"

Agent Williams: (*defiantly*) "I did what I had to do.

Elena: (*interrupting, shouting*) "You've lost your soul to power and corruption. You're a traitor to everything good and just."

Agent Williams: (*calmly*) "You can judge me all you want, Elena."

Elena stood firm, her gaze unwavering, as she confronted the man she had known as Agent Williams. The room seemed to shrink around them, suffused with tension.

Elena: (*with resolve*) " The Council of Shadows will fall, and every life harmed will be avenged. I promise you that, Mr. Samuel Harrington."

Agent Williams looked at Elena, his eyes a tableau of shock and confusion.

Elena: "Are you shocked, Mr. Harrington? Wondering how I got to know about you? You are a serpent hiding in plain sight, filled with vicious thoughts. I know everything that Richard Mercer knows. I suppose he knows very well about you, as he's the one doing everything for you upon your discreet orders. No one knows who you are. The politicians are unaware of the brainchild behind the Council of Shadows. They are just puppets dancing to your tunes."

Mr. Harrington: "You overestimate your position, Elena. Knowing fragments of information doesn't grant you true comprehension. The Council of Shadows is a necessity, a force that ensures stability in an otherwise chaotic world. The politicians dance, as you put it, not to my tunes but to the rhythms of order that we provide."

Elena: "Fuelled by relentless ambition to control the government and access privileged information, you hatched a sinister plan. Your resentment towards those who judged you based on your appearance became a driving force, pushing you to seek a transformative solution, not to provide stability. Your vision was clear—you yearned to become a formidable presence, both mentally and physically."

Mr. Harrington's face contorted with a mixture of disdain and suppressed rage as Elena laid bare the motivations behind his actions.

Mr. Harrington: "Ambition is the cornerstone of progress, and power is the currency of influence. What you label as resentment is merely the fuel that propels individuals like me to break free from the shackles of mediocrity."

He leaned forward, his eyes narrowing with intensity.

Mr. Harrington: "Transformation is not for the faint hearts. The world bows to strength, and I intend to wield it. Judgments based on appearances are the feeble attempts of the myopic to halt the march of those destined for greatness."

Harrington maintained an air of arrogance, deliberate quest for dominance in a world that he believed owed him recognition.

Elena: "Is that the reason why the ingenious CEO of Quantum Nexus Technologies, Mr. Harrington, used his brilliance to transfer his consciousness into Agent Williams's mind?"

Samuel Harrington (in disguise of Agent Williams), maintaining his facade of calm, responded with a sly smile. He revealed his malevolent machinations to Elena. The air was heavy with the weight of his words as he spoke with a cold confidence.

Harrington, leaned back in his chair, a sinister smirk playing on his lips.

"You should be glad that your uncle was among the fortunate few in my successful mind control experiments; otherwise, his fate would have been different. He did not realize his true potential," Harrington sneered. "An ex- military man with that kind of skills and reputation, I did what he could not achieve - the power to control the government. I seek pride in what I have achieved. I have a greater vision – A vision to bring the chaotic world to order."

The room seemed to close in around Elena as the gravity of Samuel Harrington's twisted ambitions sank in. She faced not just a man but a malevolent force, a puppet master entwined with the darkest corners of power. The revelation left Elena with a chilling understanding of the depth of the adversary she faced. Her eyes flashed with a mixture of fury and disbelief as Samuel Harrington callously laid bare his malevolent motives. She could hardly fathom the audacity with which he spoke, rationalizing his heinous actions as if they were noble pursuits.

Elena: "You're a monster," she seethed, her voice trembling with a mix of anger and revulsion. "Exploiting people, trafficking children, and justifying it with some twisted sense of noble achievement. There's nothing noble in what you're doing. You're just a parasite feeding off the misery of others."

Samuel Harrington chuckled, a hollow sound that echoed in the dimly lit room. "Noble? nobility is a facade created by those in power to justify their own sins. I merely embraced the reality of this world. When it comes to child trafficking, I don't see it that way", he added.

His tone disturbingly composed, "Survival demands tough choices. These children served for greater purpose. I'm ensuring their optimal development so that their potential is fully utilized in profitable way.

Everyone is an opportunist, so I used it against them, using your uncle. Everyone benefited from what I have done."

Elena's eyes widened at the callousness with which he spoke of exploiting innocent lives. The revelation of child trafficking, masked behind a veil of false benevolence, painted a grotesque picture of the man before her.

Elena's fists clenched at her sides, her resolve deepening. "Your so-called benefits are built on the suffering of innocent lives."

She took a deliberate step closer, her eyes narrowing as defiance burned like wildfire within them. Her voice, sharp and unyielding, cut through the tense air like a blade.

"You may have stolen my uncle's identity," she began, her words laced with venom. "and framed my brother for molestation, but I will not let you taint their character any further."

Her first clenched at her sides as she leaned forward, her voice dropping to a low, dangerous whisper." your precious undercover agent? The one who orchestrated the lies against my brother?. She's my captive now." she could see it- the flicker of alarm in Samuel Harrington's usually composed expression. It was fleeting, but she seized on it, a vindicated smile tugging at the corner of her lips.

"You thought you could destroy my family with your schemes, but you underestimated me." She spat, taking another step closer, her tone rising with righteous fury. "I will expose you, Samuel, For the abomination you truly are. Every dirty secret, every crime you've tried to bury-it's all coming to light. And when it does, the world will see you for the monster you are."

Samuel's jaw tightened, his calm facade starting to crack under the weight of her unrelenting gaze.

Elena, undeterred, retorted, "Your arrogance blinds you. There's always a way to dismantle a corrupt empire and I found it."

Elena: "In case you were wondering, I've apprehended all those corrupt politicians and businessmen who were your accomplices in the nefarious Council of Shadows. The game is over."

As Elena left the room, the air lingered with a sense of impending confrontation, a clash between the malevolence of Samuel Harrington and the unwavering determination of a woman ready to defy the shadows that plagued her world.

Harrington leaned back, still wearing that insidious smirk. "You don't even comprehend the scale of the game I'm playing."

20

The New Beginnings

In a bold and historic manoeuvre that would leave an indelible mark on the city's annals, the rebel group undertook a perilous mission to breach the foreboding incubator centre. Within its confines, where the purity of infants becomes a victim to heartless experimentation, a colossal screen lights up, displaying the grim particulars of these captive babies. The depths of their exploitation are laid bare, and the veil is lifted on the identities of their unsuspecting parents.

Carlos, propelled by a potent blend of rage and resolve, issues swift commands to his team. "We need to reach out to the parents immediately and rescue the auctioned children. Malik, get your team on it. Kevin, gather the necessary intel on these scientists and doctors involved in these abominable experiments. We can't let them escape justice."

As the oppressive figures behind these heinous acts are apprehended, the rebel group sets into motion a plan to expose the malevolent operations that have shrouded the city in darkness.

Meanwhile, in a coordinated assault reminiscent of a high-stakes mission, Malik Khan, Kevin Miller and their teams pinpoint the groups scattered across different regions who acquired the children through despicable auctions. The rebels, shrouded in the stealth of their advanced suits and aided by relentless drones, invade the territories of these child traffickers with a singular purpose — to rescue the infants.

As the rescue operations unfold, Elena and her team execute a breathtaking display of justice. The perpetrators, including the newly appointed mayor, the education minister (Mr. Smith), the health minister, the tech security head (Richard Mercer), and the elusive Samuel Harrington, and all other responsible members are found hanging from the city's tallest skyscraper owned by the government.

The public watches in awe and horror as the live execution is broadcasted on a colossal billboard, the rebel group masked and representing the force against tyranny.

Elena steps forward on the screen, exposing Samuel Harrington's malevolent role through his Quantum Nexus Technologies company, unraveling the sinister collusion between the corporation and the government to manipulate the unsuspecting public. The city, now witnessing the unmasking of their oppressors, stands on the precipice of a new era. Elena's voice resounding through the air as she exposes the nefarious actions of the Council of Shadows and Samuel Harrington.

Elena: "Citizens of Aurorium, today marks the end of a dark chapter in our history. For too long, our lives have been manipulated by a shadowy council, a puppet master pulling the strings from behind the scenes. The so-called Child Planning Law was nothing more than a smokescreen, a cover for the heinous crimes orchestrated by the Council of Shadows."

A hushed murmur ripples through the crowd as people exchange bewildered glances, realizing the depth of deception that had ensnared their lives.

Elena continues with unwavering determination: "Samuel Harrington, the mastermind behind this malevolence, used his influence to dictate policies, all the while concealing the true agenda — child trafficking. Innocent lives, our children, were auctioned like commodities, their futures determined not by dreams and aspirations, but by a sinister calculus of skillsets."

The crowd, once unaware of the dark underbelly of their society, listens intently as Elena lays bare the extent of the conspiracy.

Elena: "You need to know the true colors of our politicians and businessmen who are controlling us through their technology. Quantum Nexus Technologies, under the secretive influence of Samuel Harrington, achieved a stranglehold on government projects, embedding its technology into the very fabric of the state apparatus."

Elena: "Today, we cast aside the veil of deception. The Council of Shadows, Samuel Harrington and every corrupt official complicit in this scheme will face justice. Our children, our future, will be free from the shackles of this insidious manipulation. Together, we reclaim our city from the shadows that sought to control it."

As Elena's words resonate through the city, a wave of realization and defiance spreads among the populace. The revelation sparks a collective determination to dismantle the shadows that had manipulated their lives for far too long.

The sleek and lethal drones, ascend to the summits of the towering skyscrapers where the corrupt politicians and businessmen dangle as a macabre display of justice around the building. As they reach the zenith, the drones align themselves with a precision reminiscent of a choreographed dance.

Upon Elena's directive, the drones stand poised for action. A tense stillness grips the crowd, and the malevolent individuals perched atop the building tremble with fear.

Elena, observing the structure, commands, "Engage."

An expectant quiet settles over the scene as the drones, bearing both symbolic weight and retribution, release a barrage of precisely aimed flames on all sides of the building. The figures suspended against the city's backdrop are swallowed by an otherworldly blaze, their destiny sealed by the unyielding pursuit of justice.

The fiery spectacle paints the sky with an ominous glow, casting long shadows on the city below. The public, witnessing this display of comeuppance, is caught between horror and catharsis. The flames dance and crackle, symbolizing the cleansing of a city tainted by corruption and malice.

As the drones release their fiery payload on all sides of the building, a surreal cascade of broken glass and crimson rain descends upon the city streets below. The shards, remnants of shattered windows and frames, twirl and dance in the air, catching the fiery glow from above. The macabre ballet of destruction is accompanied by the haunting symphony of crackling flames and the distant screams of a city in chaos.

The blood, an unfortunate consequence of the aerial execution, mingles with the shards, painting the concrete canvas below in dark hues. It drips like a morbid rain, leaving a gruesome trail that traces the final moments of those who once wielded power with impunity.

The ordinary citizens, caught in the crossfire of justice, watch in a mix of horror and awe. The ground beneath becomes a tableau of the city's struggle for redemption, where the cost of freedom is measured in shattered glass and spilled blood. The rebellion's retaliation against the corrupt elite unfolds above them, leaving an indelible mark on the urban landscape.

Elena, masked in the digital anonymity of rebellion, watches stoically as the drones complete their fiery task. The billowing smoke ascends, carrying with it the sins of the powerful and the cries of the oppressed. The drones, having executed a form of aerial justice, return to their vigil, silent sentinels against the remnants of tyranny. The city, now marked by the scars of its tumultuous rebirth, stands poised for a new chapter in its history.

The rebellion group, under the leadership of Malik Khan, Kevin Miller and Carlos infiltrated the clandestine territories of the child trafficking syndicate with military precision.

Kevin Miller, Malik Khan, and Carlos, ex-military veterans, had seamlessly integrated into the everyday life of Aurorium city, adopting the guises of ordinary citizens to conceal their true identities. Each had a unique cover story to navigate through the complex web of the city's populace, all the while carrying the weight of their past training and experiences. They come in together for the rescue mission.

Drones, equipped with advanced surveillance and rebels in stealth suits scouted the area, relaying real-time information to the rebel command centre.

The auctioned children were kept in a heavily guarded facility, their innocence juxtaposed against the sinister operations surrounding them. The rebels, clad in state-of-the-art stealth suits, moved with silent determination through the shadows of the night.

Carlos Gomez, the tactical strategist of the group, gathered the team around a holographic display. His fingers danced across the interface, highlighting key entry points and vulnerabilities in the traffickers' defenses.

Carlos: "Alright, team, our best shot is here, at the warehouse entrance. Surveillance indicates minimal security during the night shift. Our window of opportunity is small, so we need to move fast and stay sharp."

Kevin: "I'll disable their surveillance systems. Once that's done, we'll have a limited window to get in undetected."

Carlos nodded, acknowledging the importance of precise coordination.

Carlos: "Once inside, we locate the holding area. Our priority is to extract the children and gather evidence against these traffickers. Be prepared for anything; we're stepping into the lion's den."

The team members exchanged determined glances, readying themselves for the perilous mission ahead.

With synchronized coordination, the rebels launched a multi-pronged assault. Drones engaged in electronic warfare, disabling security systems and creating diversions, while rebels on the ground neutralized guards with swift and silent strikes.

Malik Khan, leading a team of elite rebels, breached the facility's main entrance. The hallways echoed with the sounds of subdued alarms and the muffled footsteps of the rebellion, a stark contrast to the chaos unfolding outside.

As they reached the secured area where the children were held, the rebels encountered fierce resistance from the traffickers. A sophisticated hand-to- hand combat ensued, with the rebels using advanced weaponry and martial skills to subdue the traffickers without causing harm to the rescued children. Kevin Miller's team, specializing in cyber warfare, hacked into the facility's mainframe to locate the records of the auctioned children.

Simultaneously, they sent alerts to the parents of these children, notifying them of the imminent rescue.

The children, frightened and disoriented, were gently ushered out of their confinement by rebels wearing masks to conceal their identities. Each child was assigned to a rebel, forming a human shield as they navigated through the remaining resistance.

In a strategic retreat, the rebels secured the rescued children in specially designed vehicles equipped with advanced life-support systems. As they left the enemy territory, the rebel drones continued to provide cover, ensuring a safe passage back to Aurorium city.

Meanwhile, Dr. Michael, opened the portal between the two worlds to travel back to Aurorium city. Chloe and Jann, along with their new born, are ready to walk through the portal. The baby, wrapped in a soft blanket, gurgled as if sensing the extraordinary journey about to unfold. Dr. Michael, with a reassuring smile, operated the holographic controls.

"Are you ready for this incredible journey back home?" Dr. Michael asked the baby, his eyes reflecting the excitement of the moment.

Chloe, holding the baby protectively, nodded. "We trust you, Dr. Michael."

The room hummed with the faint, otherworldly energy of the portal, casting an ethereal glow that played upon the faces of Dr. Helen and Dr. Michael. They stood near the swirling vortex, its mysterious depths concealing a passage between worlds.

Dr. Helen, with a mix of melancholy and fondness, addressed Dr. Michael as he prepared to usher along with Chloe, Jann, and their new born through the interdimensional gateway.

Dr. Helen: "Dr. Michael, the work you've done has been extraordinary. Opening these portals to connect worlds is beyond our wildest dreams. None of this would have been possible without your dedication and brilliance. You've helped bridge the gap between Ethereal Nexus and Earth in ways we never thought possible."

Dr. Michael, a touch of wistfulness in his eyes, responded: "I've always believed in pushing the boundaries of what's possible. And now, it's time to go back home."

Chloe: "Dr. Helen, we can't thank you enough for what you've done for us. Our little one will grow up with the magic of two worlds."

Jann: "You've given us a chance for a life we never thought possible. We'll forever be grateful."

Dr. Helen, smiling warmly, hugged Chloe: "It was nice meeting you Chloe."

As the portal closed behind Dr. Michael, Chloe, Jann, and their new born, the room returned to its ordinary state, but the echoes of a magical connection lingered, promising a future where the boundaries between worlds would continue to blur.

The family stepped into the radiant gateway, and in an instant, the scene changed. The serene landscapes of planet Earth replaced the familiar sights of Aurorium city.

The portal had successfully transported Chloe, Jann, and their new-born across the vast expanse of the universe.

Dr. Evan: (waiting for them) "Welcome back Dad. Hugs his father, Dr. Michael, "We won the fight" he declared, a glint of accomplishment in his eyes.

Parents, long separated from their children due to the nefarious activities of the child trafficking syndicate, were awaiting the return of their precious ones. Amid the flickering lights, parents anxiously waited in a designated area. A huge sophisticated aircraft landed. The door swung open, revealing a group of relieved and tearful children, guided by rebels in stealth suits.

The moment of reunion was powerful, as parents rushed forward to embrace their long-lost children tagged with the names of their parents for identification. Tears flowed freely, and the room echoed with a mix of joy and sorrow. As the room filled with the sounds of laughter, sobs, and heartfelt conversations, it became a symbol of resilience against the darkness that had plagued Aurorium city. The rebellion had not only saved lives but had restored the hope of families torn apart by a sinister web of child trafficking.

In the wake of the rebellion's triumph, a symbolic transformation unfolded over the city of Aurorium. The towering structures, once ominous symbols of the Council of Shadows' control, were destined for a dramatic demise.

The rebel forces, with fierce determination demolished all the government's tallest skyscrapers. Each structure crumbled like a house of cards, succumbing to explosions that reverberated through the city.

As the dust settled, a profound change occurred. The cityscape, once dominated by the oppressive shadows cast by the skyscrapers, was now bathed in the warm glow of star light. The rays streamed through the spaces where the once-mighty structures stood, casting long-awaited sunshine on the streets below.

The citizens, emerging from the shadows of the past, looked up in awe and disbelief. The symbolism was potent—their city, once shrouded in darkness, was now illuminated by the triumph of justice. The rebellion had not only dismantled the physical structures that represented oppression but had also shattered the metaphorical darkness that had gripped Aurorium.

Elena, watching the scene unfold from a vantage point, felt a surge of pride and relief. The radiant bright light from the Ceti (A star like sun in the Ethereal Nexus), now unobstructed, reflected in her eyes, mirroring the hope she harboured for a new era. The rebel victory wasn't just about tearing down buildings; it was about tearing down the walls of tyranny and ushering in a dawn of freedom.

The people, sensing the transformation, gathered in the streets below. They cheered, hugged, and celebrated under the newfound starlight. The city echoed with the sounds of joy, a stark contrast to the silence imposed by the Council of Shadows. Meanwhile, Elena's squad, cloaked in stealth suits resembling airborne robots, touched down silently behind her.

Elena, addressing the crowd, proclaimed, "Today, we not only bring down the physical structures of oppression but also let the light of truth and justice shine upon our city. Let this be a reminder that no darkness can withstand the power of a united people".

With immense pride and passion, Elena lifts her hand into a fist and declares, "Our city is ours—all of ours." The crowd follows suit, raising their fists in unison and cheering.

The symbolism of the fallen skyscrapers and the emerging sunlight resonated deeply with the citizens. It marked the end of an era of secrecy and control and heralded the beginning of a transparent, just, and free Aurorium. The rebellion's victory was etched not just in the ruins of the old but in the bright promise of new beginnings.

Deep within the heart of an impenetrable forest, concealed beneath the thick canopy, a fortified underground facility housed the true architect of Aurorium's unrest. The guards, loyal to the core, patrolled the perimeter with military precision. While the disguised version of Harrington killed in Aurorium, the real puppeteer schemed in the darkness, preparing for a resurgence that would shake the very foundations of the city.

As the wind whispered through the leaves, an eerie calm enveloped the hidden facility. Samuel Harrington, a white male in 50s, in a futuristic wheelchair. With glasses perching on his deformed nose. Notably, his teeth appear visibly, adding to the distinctive aspect of his countenance. Screens flickered with reports, and the hum of machinery underscored the atmosphere. Mr. Harrington watched the events in Aurorium unfold from his secure bunker.

His eyes, sharp and calculating, scanned over maps and surveillance feeds. The city he once controlled now writhed in the turmoil of rebellion. A subtle smile played on his lips — a predator patiently waiting for the right moment to reclaim what he believed was rightfully his.

In the heart of a high-security facility, a figure lies suspended in a state of eerie stillness within a sleek, glass containment unit. The transparent walls gleam beneath the cold, sterile lights, while advanced systems monitor every heartbeat, every breath, and every subtle shift. The environment inside is controlled with surgical precision, designed to preserve life—or perhaps to create it.

Elena Rodriguez, lying dormant, waiting. A mere pawn in Samuel Harrington's vast, shadowy game. The hum of advanced machinery fills the air, embodying the unsettling quiet of an artificial life paused in time, its purpose yet to unfold.

Samuel Harrington, a calculating mastermind lurking in the shadows, watches the clone with a cold intensity. His fingers tap rhythmically on the armrest of his wheelchair, as he imagines the moment when his plan will finally unfold, sending ripples of chaos through the rebel forces of Aurorium. Little do they know, they are only scratching the surface of a far deeper, far more dangerous game.

His gaze shifts from the containment unit to the monitors tracking Elena's clone, and a cruel smile creeps across his lips. "I let you enjoy your hollow victory," he muses, his voice laced with disdain. "Do you think Richard holds all the secrets? He knows only what I allow him to. Your so-called triumph is nothing but an illusion, Elena. Prepare yourself. The true battle is about to begin, and the darkest corners of your own soul will be your next challenge. The game has only just started."

Acknowledgments and Thank You

Dear Reader,

Thank you for embarking on this journey through Rebels of Aurorium. Writing this story has been a labor of love, and I'm deeply grateful for your time and imagination as you explored the world and characters within these pages. Your support means more than words can express, and it is readers like you who bring life to the stories I create.

If you enjoyed this novel—or even if you have constructive feedback—I would be truly honored if you could take a moment to leave a review on Amazon.

Your thoughts not only help me grow as a writer but also assist other readers in discovering this book. Every review, no matter how brief, makes an enormous difference and contributes to the success of this work.

I'd also love to hear from you directly! Feel free to connect with me on Facebook / Instagram @ snagam03, where you can share your thoughts, ask questions, or simply chat about the story.

Thank you once again for being part of this adventure. Your support and feedback inspire me to keep creating, and I look forward to sharing more stories with you in the future.

Warm regards,

Satya Nagam

Author of *Rebels of Aurorium*